ON THE THRESHOLD OF TRANSFORMATION

DAILY MEDITATIONS *for* MEN

Other Books by Richard Rohr

Adam's Return:
The Five Promises of Male Initiation

Contemplation in Action

Everything Belongs:
The Gift of Contemplative Prayer

From Wild Man to Wise Man:
Reflections on Male Spirituality

Job and the Mystery of Suffering

The Naked Now:
Learning to See as the Mystics See

Quest for the Grail

Soul Brothers:
Men in the Bible Speak to Men Today

Things Hidden:
Scripture as Spirituality

ON THE THRESHOLD OF TRANSFORMATION

DAILY MEDITATIONS for MEN

RICHARD ROHR

Compiled and selected by Joe Durepos and Tom McGrath

LOYOLAPRESS.
A JESUIT MINISTRY
Chicago

LOYOLA PRESS.
A JESUIT MINISTRY

3441 N. Ashland Avenue
Chicago, Illinois 60657
(800) 621-1008
www.loyolapress.com

"Sons of Esau: Men in Our Time—and Every Time," first appeared in
Sojourners magazine as "Boys Don't Cry." Reprinted, with some adaptation,
with permission from Sojourners, (800) 714-7474, www.sojo.net.

Scripture quotations contained herein are from the *New Revised Standard
Version Bible: Catholic Edition*, copyright © 1993 and 1989 by the Division of
Christian Education of the National Council of the Churches of Christ in the
U.S.A. Used by permission. All rights reserved.

Cover image: Doug Berry/Corbis

Library of Congress Cataloging-in-Publication Data
Rohr, Richard.
    On the threshold of transformation : daily meditations for men / Richard
Rohr ; compiled, selected, and edited by Joe Durepos and Tom McGrath.
        p. cm.
    ISBN-13: 978-0-8294-3302-9
    SBN-10: 0-8294-3302-3
    1. Catholic men—Prayers and devotions. 2. Devotional calendars—
Catholic church. 3. Masculinity—Religious aspects—Christianity—
Meditations. I. Durepos, Joseph, 1955- II. McGrath, Tom, 1950- III. Title.
    BX2170.M4R64 2010
    242'.642—dc22
                                                                    2010024073

Printed in the United States of America.
10 11 12 13 14 15 16 Bang 10 9 8 7 6 5 4 3 2 1

Dedicated to Stephen J. Picha, whose tireless work and passion for the vision has moved our men's work to nine countries and thirteen regions of North America.

Contents

ix Note to the Reader

xiii Sons of Esau: Men in Our Time, Men of Every Time

1 PART 1
The Male Journey—Nature, Mythology, and the
Bigger Story

51 PART 2
The Male in Culture and Society—God, Power, and
Shame

129 PART 3
Soul Work for Men—Anger, the Shadow, Initiation,
and the Path of Descent

231 PART 4
The Paradox of Transformation—Change, Suffering,
and Freedom

303 PART 5
Male Archetypes and the Integrated Man—King,
Warrior, Magician, Lover

379 To Learn More about Richard Rohr's Ministry and
Men as Leaders and Elders (M.A.L.Es)

Note to the Reader

I approached Richard Rohr almost two years ago with an idea for a book about male spirituality that combined wisdom from all of Richard's work. I suggested to Richard that we mine his audio sets, his books, notes from his talks, unpublished materials, the daily meditations from the Center for Action and Contemplation Web site—virtually all his work that touched upon the journey of the male soul.

Richard was intrigued by the idea and encouraged me to pursue the project. He graciously gave me access to everything I asked for and needed. Previously, I've had some success selecting and compiling the wisdom of spiritual teachers. However, this project came out of an intensely personal desire to share and understand more deeply the transformative nature of Richard's work that I've found so life altering for many years.

In the mid nineties, much of what we think of as the modern men's movement had lost its energy and gone underground. Richard Rohr came along quietly with a model of male spirituality that was theologically sound and psychologically astute. He blended the great Christian spiritual tradition with the profound insights of psychology, mythology, and anthropology. He then orchestrated the creation of the "Men's Rites of Passage," a transformative experience for men of all ages. This initiation process is based on decades of Richard's study and centuries of human wisdom.

Shortly after I started work on this project, a series of misfortunes descended on me that would challenge your credulity if I were to list them. A friend suggested that I change my name from Joe to Job. I laughed, but he wasn't kidding.

Thus, I lived this book as I worked on it. I can assure you, this material is field-tested. I used the wisdom you will find within these pages to navigate the most difficult time in my life. I am a better man now than I was before. I can't say that it was good that calamity came upon me and my family, but I can say that good has come out of it.

I've seen how Richard's work has helped many men. I've also experienced firsthand, during the difficult period of putting this book together, the gift of Richard's wisdom in transforming pain and tragedy into gift and blessing. I know you will find much in this book that will help you on your journey. I should warn you, though—this is not a daily devotional. In fact, it's more of a "daily confrontational." It's not inspiring, at least not in the sentimental sense of the word. It is truthful and brave and invites us to be the same.

Richard urges men to change, and he tells us that change is hard, that suffering is involved, and that the work required is taxing and difficult. But don't get the idea that a man's journey is only a miserable slog. There's a gentle, encouraging spirit in much of what Richard says here, and it's there because Richard knows that on the other side of suffering lie wholeness and fruitfulness. And more important, he's not just a voice cheering from the sidelines. He's up around the bend, scouting the terrain, beckoning us to follow.

Richard shows men how to accept, and not rage at, the inevitable wounding of life. We can make our suffering holy by moving it into sacred space. He shows us how to look at the shadow and not be frightened by what we see, but rather to respect and even befriend what we find there. He pleads with us not to pass on our pain or inflict it on others, but rather to listen and learn from it.

Richard offers a bracing vision. On a man's journey, everything has its place. Our failures, heartbreaks, defeats, and victories; our wounds, dreams, and passions; our stops and our starts—all have a place in our story, and all have a place in our transformation from shadow men to real men. Everything has meaning, and everything belongs.

This book is an invitation and a guide. It really helps. I know. Plunge in and see for yourself.

Blessings on the journey,
Joe Durepos
Woodridge, IL
April, 2010

Sons of Esau: Men in Our Time, Men of Every Time

We are getting used to the troubling news reports of men killing their fellow workers, wives, children, or their entire families. Of course, we are appalled, and suspect that such a man must have been drunk, on drugs, or mentally ill. Often that's the case, but more often the "reason" is probably even deeper than these apparent addictions or illnesses.

I have no exact statistics, but I assume that these crimes have been on the increase since the recent economic recession—loss of jobs and all the insecurity and fear that goes with it. I surely would not want to blame such behavior on these factors only, but let me also suggest a few others at a deeper level. Men as a class appear to be "at risk," maybe even at high risk.

We certainly see this in the return of many soldiers from Iraq and Afghanistan. Last year I was invited to give a retreat to the Army Chaplain Core, and they are genuinely overwhelmed by the highest incidence of post traumatic stress disorder among their men and women. Edward Tick's influential book, *War and the Soul*, makes the case that many men were seeking some kind of initiation in joining the armed forces, only to be massively disillusioned.

After twenty years of working with men on retreats and rites of passage, in spiritual direction, and even in prison, it has sadly become clear to me how trapped the typical Western male feels. He is trapped inside, with almost no inner universe of deep meaning to heal him or guide him. Historically, this is exactly what spirituality meant by "losing your soul." It did not happen later or after death unless it first happened here.

For centuries, males have been encouraged and rewarded for living an "outer" life of performances, which are usually framed in terms of win or lose. Just listen to boys talk—they have already imbibed it, and usually with the encouragement of both dad and mom. The world of sports, contests, *American Idol*, video games, and proving oneself is most males' primary "myth," through which he frames all reality. I challenge anyone to claim that is an overstatement.

In such a worldview there are only winners or losers, no in-between, and little chance for growth or redemption once you are deemed—or deem yourself—a loser. In the West, even the gospel is taught largely in terms of a giant reward/punishment system, which I guess made sense to a primarily male clergy. This is the way we prefer to frame reality. Here there is little talk or concern for healing or growth or inner spiritual development. "Why would I need healing?" I have heard men say outright. The word itself is strange to many men; it sounds soft and needy—and this rejection is a sure-fire plan for having an absolutely huge shadow world and an unconscious agenda that calls the shots. Are ongoing political, Wall Street, and church scandals really a surprise?

By "shadow world," I simply mean all of those aspects of our own memory and hurt that remain hidden in our unconscious, those things that we're not prepared to deal with at the moment. They highly influence us, but we have no conscious control over such feelings, motivations, fears, and agendas, so they tend to do more bad than good. Spiritual healing is precisely about bringing those issues to consciousness, which is often quite painful and yet also deeply consoling.

I once suggested to a group of middle-class Catholic men that the gospel might actually be a win/win scenario between God and humanity. An obviously successful man came up to me afterward and said, "But Father, that would not even be interesting." It took away his whole motivation if life could not be framed in terms of some type of win/ lose contest—at which, not surprisingly, he saw himself as the ultimate insider and winner. American, healthy, white, heterosexual, Roman Catholic, and probably Republican. No wonder Jesus said to the outsider, "Never have I found such faith inside of Israel."

Take a typical woman, educated or uneducated, of most any race or ethnicity, and give her this agenda: "You are not to have any close friends or confidants; you are to avoid any show of need, weakness, or tender human intimacy; you may not touch other women without very good reason; you may not cry; you are not encouraged to trust your inner guidance, but only outer authorities and 'big' people; and you are to judge yourself by your roles, titles, car, house, money, and successes. People are either in your tribe, or they are a competitive threat—or of no interest!" Then tell her, "This is what it feels like to be a male, most of the time." Maleness can be a very lonely and self-defeating world.

Very few women would choose that kind of agenda. Feminism and social engineers were right when they said that the typical male in most cultures has many more options and chances for advancement. But few pointed out that they were talking primarily about outer options. After forty years of ministry with many groups at different levels, I am convinced that women have far more inner options and a richer inner life—even if equally neurotic. Men have more outer options, women have more inner; that is the norm.

In describing inner feelings and states, and in talking about what they really want and need, women have many times the vocabulary that men do. They have a much more nuanced emotional life in most cases, and in general they are more skilled at relationships than men. I have done my own survey on this one: On my visits to the local grocery store, on the street, or on a hiking trail, women I meet are three times as likely as men to say "Hello," "Pardon me," "Sorry," "Thank you," or a simple "Good morning." Many men do not even say "Excuse me" when you step out of the way for them as they barrel forward—our slowed-down version of road rage, I guess. Maybe this is simply because I am male myself, and the rules would be different if I were a woman. But it sure makes me wonder about the relational capacities—and even the relational interest—of the typical American male.

But how else would a man be expected to act if he does not know how to identify, much less know how to share, his sadness, his anger, or his endless grief—often about his own love and losses, or the world that he once dreamed would happen? In the male initiation rites we have been leading for almost fifteen years (www.malespirituality.org), one of the most surprising but revealing discoveries was that much male anger is actually male sadness. Men often have no way to know this themselves, and many probably even think of themselves as "angry men." They are often very sad men, but they have no differentiated feeling world, no vocabulary, no safe male friends, no inner space or outer setting in which to open up such a chasm of feeling—not even in their churches or with their partners.

I know I am walking on sacred ground here, but I'm going to say it: The church often does not really encourage an inner life. It substitutes belief systems and belonging systems and moral systems for interior journeys toward God. As a result the outer behavior is pretty weak as well. I would be willing to argue this position at the highest levels of Catholic hierarchy, Protestant scripture interpretation, or fundamentalist mental gymnastics.

In fact, the reason that such external hierarchy, simplistic and dualistic readings of scripture, and heady fundamentalism exist at all is primarily because of the male unwillingness to feel, to suffer, to lose, and to stand in the place of the outsider with even basic empathy. Which, of course, is exactly where Jesus stood and suffered, "even to accepting death, yes death on a cross" (Philippians 2:8). How do we dare to worship a "loser" and yet so idealize winning?

So what do we do for our men, our husbands, our fathers, sons, and brothers? First of all, it's important to note that throughout history many varied cultures, all over the world, have recognized this problem. These cultures saw that men would not go inside themselves until and unless they had to—and then it was often too late. So they guaranteed and structured an inner journey for the male somewhere between the ages of thirteen and seventeen, and it was called initiation. It likely didn't even work in most cases, but cultures knew they had to do it for the social survival of the tribe. Initiation was effective for enough men to guarantee eldership: wise men, men who moved beyond ego, control, and power into the second half of life, men with the nondualistic mind that we call wisdom.

Initiation in most cultures was done through two methods: extended solitude and silence, and ritualized sacred suffering. That was the cauldron of transformation for the male. Many cultures, in a wide variety of times and places, came to the inescapable conclusion: There was no other way.

If our churches do not find ways to validate, encourage, structure, and teach men an inner life—as opposed to mere belief systems, belonging systems, and moral systems, which the Olympics do much better!—I'm not sure what the church's reason for continued existence might be. We are failing the test with one half of the species, which means we are failing for the other half, too. Organized religion is not doing its inherent job of transforming people at any deep level.

In short, we have substituted an intellectual life for a symbolic life, a largely mental life for a life of inner meaning, and a nice Christian club for the call to a journey that males could actually respect. We can live without success, but the soul cannot live without meaning.

An important message is found in the Genesis 27 story of Jacob and Esau. Our men are like Esau, fooled by their brothers and their fathers too, and deprived of their deepest birthright. No wonder that the Esaus of our time "want to take revenge and kill" (Genesis 27:42). You cannot take away a man's soul or fail to reveal his soul to him without dire consequences for family, neighborhood, church, and society as a whole. Esau seems to eternally cry out, "Father, do you not have a blessing for me? Do you only have one blessing?" (27:38).

Notice in this famous story of Jacob and Esau that both of them are led by pure self-interest and seeking to maximize their "outer options." That is the uninitiated male in every culture, including the Hebrew culture of the Bible. Rebecca, their mother, opens up their "inner options," guides them every step of the way, protects them from one another, covers for their father, validates their cunning, and protects them from their own deceit and ambition.

Rebecca might not be perfect—in fact she isn't. But at least she has some imagination, some caring, some passion, some creativity, some risk taking, some inner intelligence, beyond the simple win or lose game of Jacob and Esau. I wonder if Jacob and Esau are not the very archetypes of win or lose, all or nothing, dualistic minds, no blessing left if you are not Jacob himself.

Could this be the very name of faith for men in our time? We need to help our men move beyond the self-defeating game of either-or, and to find the open and gracious space of the limitless, alive, and God-given world that is in-between. Where all of us live anyway.

✦ ✦ ✦

This book is the fruit of months of listening, reading, selecting, editing, and transcribing on the part of two wonderful friends, Joe Durepos and Tom McGrath. They gathered my scattered thoughts to groups of men from over a twenty-year period and put them together into 366 meditations. That is how much they care about men and about "where all of us live anyway"!

I thank them for their patience and their generosity of spirit, and together we offer these meditations for your own consideration—and healing, insight, and encouragement. Although it might sometimes feel like momentary discouragement!

We have deliberately not attached them to specific days, months, holidays, or seasons, so you can read them *when you are ready.* They won't do much good if you are not ready. Don't force yourself ahead, but only return when the last one has had time to soak in, be repelled, or drain out. I'm sure not every meditation will apply to you, nor do you need to agree with, or fight, my interpretations. Allow me to be wrong. I've turned "wrong" into an art form, and it has taken me to God. It will take you there, too.

Remember, we are all sons of Esau, always waiting for the "birthright" and still believing in the blessing.

Richard Rohr
Pentecost, 2010

PART 1

The Male Journey—Nature, Mythology, and the Bigger Story

If we don't learn to mythologize our lives, inevitably we will pathologize them.
—**Richard Rohr**

✦ Being true to our quest, we set forth on a journey to travel, to move toward a new understanding of ourselves and our place in the world.

✦ If we don't move beyond the self-referential trap of our own stories and lives, and connect with the larger story of what it means to be a man, we'll live lives of quiet desperation.

✦ It is only when we've left the safety of our known world, the world in which we feel in control, that we will discover mythology is real and true and has something profound to teach us.

✦ We need to encounter the hero within and let him lead us on the adventure of our lives.

DAY 1

THE MALE JOURNEY

At some point in time, a man needs to embark on a risky journey. It's a necessary adventure that takes him into uncertainty, and it almost always involves some form of difficulty or failure. On this journey the man learns to trust God more than he trusts a sense of right and wrong or his own sense of self-worth.

We find this story arc in countless myths, fairy tales, and legends. A man leaves the comfort of his home only to return and rediscover home and, as T. S. Eliot wrote, "know it for the first time."

We tend to take refuge in the static world of ideas and opinions, and we look for meaning in jobs and careers. Often we mistake the roles we play for authentic living. But eventually a man begins to sense that something is missing. He may experience this call to awareness as a beckoning whisper, a powerful dream, or a sudden and stark life change—but no matter how it shows up, it needs to be heeded.

Do I feel a vague call to something more? Am I willing to pay attention?

Day 2

Wanderlust

In the first half of life, a young man believes that life's truths lie elsewhere, out there, away from home—far from where he is. He is looking for his soul. In the classic male rite of passage story, the hero will often wander aimlessly, traveling with no destination in mind. He believes that new horizons will reveal his true identity, his purpose, and his vision for life. This is known as wanderlust—the desire and need to see a larger world.

Eventually, like Jacob, a man wakes up one day from his long sleep and says, "Surely the LORD is in this place—and I did not know it!" (Genesis 28:16). The big truth for men is that often we have to leave home in the first half of life before we can return home at a later stage and find our soul there.

When have I felt wanderlust? What was calling me? Where did it lead me?

Day 3

The Great Quest

The great Grail legends first appeared in Europe around 1180 and flourished until 1350. They became popular at the same time that the gospel was either not being preached or fading in importance for Christian men. The Grail stories—which emerged in German, French, and English versions—became a way for laymen to describe and understand the spiritual path in a nonacademic way.

These stories always involved a quest or journey of some type; they were genuine myth but anchored in men's reality. *Myth* refers to something that is profoundly true at the deepest levels of life. Myths of the Holy Grail reflected Christian lay spirituality at its most authentic.

Today, the great quest no longer seems real or inviting. Many of us are unsure of our spiritual goals. We have difficulty reading the meaningful patterns of our existence, and we remain unconvinced or even uninterested in our divine origins. This is a major crisis of meaning that results in a loss of hope and a lack of vision.

Do I see my life as a noble quest that brings meaning and purpose? Do I have the support I need to begin my quest? What would I need to begin today?

Day 4

The Holy Grail

In culture after culture, much has been written about blood. It holds deep, archetypal meanings in all storytelling, both as the ultimate energy of life and the ultimate symbol of death. The Eucharist speaks to this dramatically; we are taking in of the essence of another, and it speaks on a cellular, physical level. This is deeply transformative if we allow it to be. Quite simply, we become what we eat and drink.

This experience has lost some of its power. In ancient initiation rites, men sometimes drank the blood of their elders and heroes. The Eucharist has at times become an antiseptic caricature of the original Supper, complete with lace on the altar and priests dressed in silk. This distracts us from the graphic symbol: we are drinking the blood of our hero—Christ—and are now one with him. This is good stuff; if we didn't already have something like this, we would have to invent it.

If the Christian ritual of communion (Eucharist)
is part of my life, what does it mean to me?
If I don't have the eucharistic ritual, what
other form or symbol might I have for sharing
the essence of a hero?

Day 5

Vision Quest

In the classic Native American vision quest, a young man would head out to the wilderness, find a solitary place, and then wait. He didn't return home until he received his destiny and the Great Spirit gave him his true name. That name told the young man who he was and what his life's purpose would be.

Confirmation in the Christian tradition was supposed to work similarly. It was intended to give us a jolting experience of the indwelling Holy Spirit, and we often chose a name that had spiritual meaning for us at that time. It did not always coincide with finding our life vision, but still it's clear that Christian sacraments built on deep and abiding patterns of initiation.

Many of us still need to go on our vision quest and have our souls "confirmed." What many men desire—and some don't even have the language to express it—is an inner vision that tells them where they fit in the world and what they are here to do, something that is often different from what they do to pay the bills.

Have I heard my real name? What am I here on earth to do?

Day 6

A Radically Benevolent Universe

Traditional myths and stories present a benevolent universe, a hostile universe, or an indifferent universe. This is what our children seek in movies, books, and even video games; they are looking for the shape of their universe. Mature Christians should recognize that ours is a generous and benevolent universe, as described in the first chapter of Genesis. We are told that this world is not only good, safe, and on our side, but that there is Someone who is *for* us more than we are for ourselves!

This truth must be felt, understood, and drawn upon to become life-giving. The work of healthy religion is to open our eyes to see a world in which everything swirls with meaning. Theologically, you could call heaven "the transcendent inside" of everything. Heaven is not so much a place out there as it is the full depth and dynamism of things *in here*. That's why Jesus said "the kingdom of [heaven] is within you" (Luke 17:21). Heaven is an experience now before it is later and forever.

When, and in what circumstances, did I begin to understand that I'm part of a larger story?

Day 7

Everything Belongs

We can begin to understand the bigger story we are a part of when we engage with the unique Christian sense of time, process, and journey. This perception is presented beautifully in the Grail quest; it's the story of a young man searching for God and himself. Through ongoing trials and temptations, the young man pushes toward God, almost without knowing it. God leads him forward through family, failure, violence, visitors, betrayal, sexuality, nature, shadow, and vision. God comes to him "disguised as his life." The story is told in language most men can relate to, not in "churchy" language. It's a tale told with muscle, merit, and meaning.

Everything on this journey is necessary and grace filled. For the man on the quest, the universe becomes enchanting—an effect that good religion accomplishes. There are no dead ends, no wasted time, no useless characters or meaningless happenings. All has meaning, and God is in all things waiting to speak and to bless. Everything belongs once a man is on his real quest and asking the right questions.

Looking back on my life, where can I see blessing and meaning where perhaps I didn't before?

DAY 8

INTO THE WILD

Each man who embarks on a spiritual journey has to walk out into the wild and face his demons. Mark's Gospel tells us that "the Spirit . . . drove [Jesus] out into the wilderness" (1:12), which seems to indicate that we'll probably not go into our own wilderness until forced into it by circumstance. It also says that "he was with the wild beasts," and, finally, that "the angels waited on him" (1:13). So it seems that the man who is brave enough to face his demons may also encounter the better angels of his nature. The sequence is important: wild beasts first, angels second.

Shadowy material resides inside each one of us, but the man who is willing to face his own capacity for darkness will discover his deepest inner goodness and the presence of the divine within him. Some men never discover the divine presence within because they can't bring themselves to face their demons. Don't try to engineer this process or manufacture any angels. It will be done to you; just do not hate or fear the falling.

What stands in the way of my facing my inner darkness? Am I willing to walk into the wilds of my interior life without knowing what I'll find?

Day 9

A Good Day to Do Great Things

In the great legends, the hero almost always was an ordinary man with at least one tragic flaw. Like any of us, he was neither a saint nor a god, but he was willing and able to focus on his quest. Usually the goal was beyond his known abilities—and often the real goal was to encounter God, although the hero never knew this till the end.

According to legend, the Great Plains warriors would say to their sons first thing in the morning, "It is a good day to do great things." If we can't say something like this, we will not experience the quest. We need this kind of desire and expectation. We receive it from other men and also give it to other men, sometimes unknowingly. We need to allow our souls to be stirred by a magnificent ambition—something that makes us jump out of bed in the morning, that calls us to be some kind of hero in our own kind of story, even if we know we have more than one tragic flaw.

What is calling to the heroic within me? What magnificent ambition am I willing to undertake?

DAY 10

THE HERO WITHIN

There is a hero within each man, and however corny it may sound to our modern, cynical selves, we should pay attention to the voice of this hero. He says that your life is not just your own, not just a personal matter. However incomprehensible it may seem to us Western individualists, the boundaries of our lives go far beyond our particular selves. It's the job of religion to communicate this truth to us in no uncertain terms.

Most of us understand that "me" has its limits, which is why we try to dress up our lives in artificial ways. Our inner hero wants to move us beyond "just me" to "we are" and ultimately to the biblical experience of "I am." By itself, "my story" is too small. "Our story" is too clannish. But "the Story" places the individual in the truly big picture. Then "I" become one moment of the great parade that manifests God in history. In that story line, we are all hidden heroes.

What would it look like to move from "just me" to "we are"? What does it mean to move from "we are" to "I am"?

Day 11

No Geographical Solutions

Every man wants to discover something, to find what is missing here by journeying to a new place. We forget that we take the same old self to the new place. New experiences are safely tucked inside of—or excluded from—our already existing persona or worldview. I remember lying on a beach in Maui and having to admit that I was no happier there than when I was in my backyard in New Mexico.

Sometimes we refer to this as the geographical solution, the idea that we can solve our problems through an experience far from home. Encounters with the unfamiliar can indeed open new possibilities and perspectives—but only if they break through our filters and actually change us. New experiences are more often diversionary tactics.

Eventually, the young man realizes that what he is searching for cannot be found externally. Nothing outside the self can substantially change us or make us happy unless it realigns us internally.

Was there a time when I sought a geographical solution to my soul's restlessness? When was that, and what were the circumstances? When did I first realize that there are no geographical solutions?

Day 12

The Simple and the Beautiful

If he is wise, a man travels in what might be seen as a circular journey, seeking the new only to rediscover the old. The big patterns never change. He always returns to the place he started from, only now with the real meaning revealed. He experiences happiness at home base, and yet it is deeper and wider than before.

For the young man, this necessary journey is a form of re-creating the myth of the fallen and resurrected world. Albert Einstein said that, in searching for his theory of relativity, all he had before him was the conviction that whatever the big truth was, it would be both *simple and beautiful.* The young man always makes the journey complex and worrisome. If you stay on the spiritual journey, I can promise you that life will gradually become much more simple, clear, and pared down—and that is precisely what makes life beautiful!

---

*What, for me, is beautiful? And how would I
describe simplicity?*

Day 13

The Cosmic Egg

Many people of faith believe that Western civilization is in a state of spiritual emergency. People are leaving every mainline denomination in droves; only fundamentalism seems to be gathering new adherents. Many people are living with massive disillusionment. The problem is that we have lost our symbolic universe of meaning—the "cosmic egg" has been broken, and a new one is still waiting to be formed. The coherent world in which things used to fit together and make sense has been shattered. *The soul can live without answers, but it cannot live without meaning.*

We are desperately seeking a mythic universe in which to stand and make our lives relevant and heroic. Frankly, I am wondering more and more if cosmology itself, with a truly cosmic Christ, is not the new—and oldest—mythology. Certainly this universe that we are part of is the one single thing we all share. It situates us inside immense meaning and beauty, but we need a touch of the scientist-mystic soul to allow this meaning and beauty to affect us fully.

What evidence have I seen of the rupture of the cosmic egg—the coherent universe—in my life?

Day 14

When We Don't Mythologize, We Pathologize

When people lose a meaningful story line for their lives, they disintegrate both personally and culturally. A mythic universe holds the individual and group soul together, by giving it purpose and meaning. It operates in our unconscious for the most part, but when it breaks down, sickness, addiction, neuroses, desperation, and suicide prevail.

We lost our ability to appreciate myth around the time of the Enlightenment. Nature, religion, mystery, and ritual all became passé. We're now living in a post-Christian era dominated by rationalism, which desires above all to understand, change, and control everything.

But if we don't mythologize, and give greater meaning to our actions, we will almost always pathologize and see everything as wrong, absurd, or requiring a change or fix before we can be happy.

What does it mean to mythologize my life, and why is it so important to do so?

Day 15

The Meaning of Symbol

In much world mythology, the sword first has a positive meaning: a person's ability to be discriminating and decisive. The sword helps a man separate his feelings from the issues at hand. It helps him name and maintain appropriate boundaries. A man with a sword knows who he is and who he isn't, and what is worth protecting.

The sword also has borne a negative meaning: killing and death. Spiritually speaking, however, it's necessary to kill or at least distinguish the dark side, the small, egocentric self. Also, for a man to be born, boyhood and "keeping all my options open" must die, and this is painful, especially in a culture that encourages perpetual adolescence. So even in its negative sense the sword can become a symbol of the healthy warrior and an expression of his spiritual side. It does not always have to mean violence or rage.

When have I known that something in my life had come to an end? Where did I find the strength to acknowledge this truth?

Day 16

The Quest(ion)

The male quest is always about clarifying the questions. This is why we need a discriminating sword; with it we hack through the confusion and distractions of life to find our real name, our real self. The words *quest* and *question* share the same root; a man will not go on a quest until he begins searching for the right questions. I think the world is tired of religious men with loads of answers for everything.

It is by learning the questions slowly and attentively that we are drawn into the depth of things and, frankly, the sadness of things, and into compassion. We won't find very meaningful answers if we haven't asked the right questions; it also helps if we have lived without answers for a while. But we tend to settle for formulas, clichés, and prevailing opinions instead of any real wisdom. I am afraid this is why our public discourse is so dualistic, angry, and unhelpful. We really can do much better.

What is the deepest unasked question of my life?
What questions am I being asked to live with
right now?

DAY 17

FATHER HUNGER

There's an emptiness that results from the absence of a father's energy. This ache for the father grew acute during the industrial revolution, when fathers began leaving for work early each day and returning home tired at night. Now it continues with fathers working on the road or commuting to downtown offices.

When the father and son do not have sufficient shoulder-to-shoulder time, healthy masculine energy does not pass from father to son. If the son does not find a healthy way to heal or compensate for that lack of energy, the void will fill with insecurity, depression, rage, and more.

Without positive modeling from man to boy, the grown-up boy may find it difficult to relate to others. He may experience sadness that can turn debilitating by midlife. He may have trouble with self-confidence, sound judgment, and reading life's situations correctly. He may not understand his own feelings or how to empathize with others. He may never learn how to cry, because he is disconnected from his deepest feelings. These lessons call for mentoring that only men can do.

Where can I go as a man to find healthy ways to heal the grief of father-hunger? What can I do so that my sons don't experience this same sense of loss?

DAY 18

FINDING YOUR DELIVERY SYSTEM

If a man really wants to know what he was put on earth to do, he should ask this question: "What if doing what I was created to do means not earning as much money?" If we're not willing to take a decrease in salary, we're probably not ready to go on the quest.

Imagine the dilemma of Peter and Andrew, whose only livelihood was fishing. Jesus tells them to leave their nets, and "immediately they left their nets and followed him" (Matthew 4:20). They had to make a risky move from mere occupation to real vocation. Most of us think that blatant sins keep us from the journey, but *very often it is good things that keep us from the better or best things*—good things such as conformity and a comfortable job.

If I were one of the twelve apostles, called to leave all I know to follow a stranger into a completely uncertain future, how would I respond?

DAY 19

MENTORS

One of the greatest difficulties for men today is the lack of suitable guides to help us along the journey. There are so few mentors who have made the journey themselves and have come back ready to guide us. We need father figures of some sort, men who have traversed a little more of the journey—and who have come out the other side happy and wise.

Today we tend to have more elderly people than actual elders who have something to teach us. As men, we long for mentors—at every stage of the journey—who are believable and reliable.

Who are my mentors? Whom do I mentor?

Day 20

Life Precedes Doctrine

Nothing in the Bible says that primary authority lies in the Scriptures or in doctrines themselves. These serve only to point beyond themselves to the hard facts of reality, life itself, and from there to authentic encounters with God.

The point of Scripture, and all sacred texts, is to point us toward the very thing that the characters themselves did. Whether Moses or Muhammad, the prophet Ezekiel, the Buddha, or anybody else—they had to take responsibility for what life dished out to them. Maybe sacred texts invited them onto the journey, but usually it was some experience of encounter itself that kept them there and gave them their passion and direction. Ideas don't change people on a deep level; encounter with the "other" changes people.

Later, when returning from their real-life journey, these great figures often found confirmation or great consolation in those Scriptures or doctrines. Never let belief systems be an actual barrier to loving, living, or knowing God for yourself.

How has sacred text been a part of my life? In what ways do I hope to enter those sacred stories now?

Day 21

The Deeper Questions

Education, both secular and religious, has for many years given people easy answers to questions they weren't even asking. People accept the answers too quickly, and those answers sink in about an inch deep. To make matters worse, some of those shallow answers become the truths that people spout for the rest of their lives. This kind of easily won knowledge can pass away as quickly as it came. Why is this? It is knowledge we did not thirst for or long for.

Sometimes we use the easy answers to avoid the real questions. Because we know the answer already, we stop searching. We sit down and remain stationary rather than stepping into the difficult journey of hard-won faith.

Many men are no longer on a journey. They've accepted the easy answers before they've struggled with the deep questions.

What easy answers have I examined honestly and then kicked out of my way on this spiritual path? What easy answers still allow me to avoid struggle and longing?

DAY 22

NATURE IS GOD'S FIRST SCRIPTURE

In the future, morality will come primarily from the earth and the very nature of the cosmos, not from religion (which hasn't done a very good job up to now). This one planet on which all of us stand will tell us that we must live simple lives, and that we must live reverent lives that produce and create instead of merely consume and destroy. And if creation itself is the body of God—the visible revelation of who God is—won't we find ourselves at home again?

This concept of morality and God is not a form of earth worship. But it does accept the earth as a part of God's self-expression, a revelation of the divine nature, and therefore something to be honored, respected, and attended with mind and heart and every physical sense.

Nature itself is God's first, oldest, and clearest Scripture.

What have I already learned about God from the natural world? How can my life become simpler and more reverent?

DAY 23

CREATION AND COMMUNION

We've got to give back to the material world its power, its importance, its soul, and its sacredness. This whole earth is indeed a land of enchantment. St. Francis would not step on a little worm knowingly but would pick it up and place it by the side of the road.

St. Francis of Assisi was the first Christian to address creatures as "brother" and "sister." Animals, sun, moon, plants, and the very air were soulful and mutual subjects for him, not just objects for his use. The importance of this cannot be overemphasized in a world that severely suffers from what the author Richard Louv calls "nature deficit disorder." We have forgotten how to read and reverence God's first revelation to us.

Such reverential seeing will lead to the beginnings of true enlightenment: love for that tree, joy in that animal, awareness in that breeze, and God in that pain. Soon you will wonder what this communion is that passes back and forth between you and everything else. It is the largest and the very best communion of saints.

With what parts of creation do I experience communion?

Day 24

The Great Chain of Being

We take our life on this earth too lightly. We allow and cooperate with the destruction of God's creation, for which we are responsible as stewards. One of the more terrifying aspects of today's world is how comfortable we've become with killing people, animals, all growing things, and the earth itself. What does this say about our level of spiritual maturity? We destroy while surely intuiting that killing is the antithesis of love and respect for the God of life.

We know that the divine is revealed in all created beauty and wisdom around us. Yet we who are supposed to be higher in the great chain of being do not always appear to be so but are often quite self-centered. Ultimately, life is one, and our attitude toward one part affects our attitude in general. St. Paul says that we should treat the lesser parts "with greater respect" (1 Corinthians 12:23). When any segment of the great chain of life is disrespected and destroyed, the entire chain is broken and the sacred everywhere is lost.

What is my personal experience
with creation as sacred?

DAY 25

THERE IS ONLY THE SUPERNATURAL

Through much of Western history, a strong notion has prevailed: that the world was divided between the natural and the supernatural. And often, those of us of a religious viewpoint opted for the supernatural. We saw the natural as something we needed to rise above, or get beyond. We spent so much effort trying to fly up to the supernatural that we forgot what the medieval theologians said: that grace can only build on nature. They are not separate, but inform and reveal each other! For people who have learned to see, everything is supernatural.

We need to remain solidly grounded in our own nature, in ordinary events, and in real-life situations, so that divine grace has something real and good to build on. The scandal and disappointment of Jesus was that he looked like everybody else; he was a bit too earthy and real—in fact, at times he didn't seem very spiritual at all. If he had looked more supernatural, we never would have killed him.

How do I really feel about my natural life?
When have I tried to reject it in favor of
something more supernatural?

DAY 26

WHO ARE YOU REALLY?

For most men, midlife is usually the last chance to make any real change. If a man has not taken any great risks by the time he's fifty, chances are he's too entrenched in his day-to-day life to make radical changes.

This may be the reason why many men have a midlife crisis—it's God shaking the tree one last time and challenging us. Will you give up the illusion? Will you stop being just who you think you're supposed to be and finally be who you really are?

Have I reached any sort of crisis point in my life?
If so, what are the opportunities for
change and discovery?

Day 27

Too Early for the Journey

Many Eastern traditions did not allow a man to study spirituality until he was in his midthirties at the earliest. Carl Jung imposed similar restrictions for students at his institute in Zurich. In the Catholic Church, a man cannot become a bishop until he is thirty-five.

There is collective masculine wisdom that says if a man sets out on the journey too early, he has probably not loved enough, not failed enough, and not suffered enough to know the terrain in even rudimentary ways. He will more likely use God or religion for his own career or ego advancement, while swearing that he's not. He will possess smug and totally untested answers that just happen to benefit his private success story. Early in life a man is still building his own tower and surely not ready to help anybody else build theirs. This is exactly why a demanding initiation was deemed necessary for the male in almost all early cultures; they understood human nature.

How have love, failure, and suffering informed my personal development up until now?

Day 28

Protecting Your Gold

"To all those who have, more will be given, and they will have an abundance; but from those who have nothing, even what they have will be taken away" (Matthew 25:29).

Until we have discovered our own identity and gifts, we tend to idealize and imitate others and put them on pedestals. And we hand over our power to them instead of finding it within ourselves and drawing from our own resources. It's a kind of infatuation (*ignis fatuus* or "false fire") that will eventually disappoint or disillusion us. We also fall in love with people who appear to hold the power that we ourselves want: physical attractiveness, money, position, talent, or influence. We worship others for what they do for us temporarily, and in doing this we miss the value and foundation that we ourselves possess. Sooner or later, we will have to withdraw our gold from this unstable security box. If not, we will remain permanently poor.

Where is my gold right now?

Day 29

Giving Away Your Gold

Jesus often instructed his disciples not to talk about the
wonders they had seen him perform; he also would say to
a person he had healed, "Do not talk about this to anyone."
When we at the Center for Action and Contemplation take
men through initiation rites or other intense experiences,
we tell them not to talk about what has happened to them,
not even to their wives, for maybe a couple of weeks. We
say, "Don't give away your gold until it is really *your* gold!"

Once you verbalize something, it's as if you have done
a freeze-frame, stopping it at that level, and this often stops
further growth. You sort of capture it in words and, frankly,
should expect little more from it. It becomes more a posses-
sion of the ego than an ongoing experience. The unfolding
and deeper synthesis that becomes true gold, your own gold,
integrated gold for good, never happens, and you lose even
the bit that you had. *So never hand over your deepest experiences until they have become integrated as your very own.*

What do I usually do with my gold?

Day 30

Some Call This Enlightenment

In classic spiritual stories from all over the world, the male seeker moves through several levels, today referred to as levels of consciousness. He travels from simple consciousness, to complex consciousness, and finally to enlightened consciousness, which looks surprisingly simple again.

The first simplicity and the second simplicity are, in fact, completely different. The first simplicity is necessarily naïve and inexperienced. Also, a man in the first stage must split his life—the natural from the spiritual, the light from the shadow, the problems from the easier times. But when he comes to enlightened consciousness and that second simplicity, he has learned to include, accept, and forgive the negatives, the problems, and the contradictions that were revealed in the middle stage.

We could say it this way too: as we grow older, we live, love, sin, fail, forgive, read, wait, struggle, and search, presuming that we have to get it right all by ourselves. Finally we discover both the Source and the guidance, and when we place our trust in that larger reality, life becomes simple again.

How would I accurately describe the stages I've gone through?

Day 31

Where the Soul Leads

"Nothing is covered up that will not be uncovered, and nothing secret that will not become known" (Matthew 10:26).

What is the value of talking about moving through different levels of consciousness? Is this just new psychobabble? One way to look at it is this: Because we can't make sense of things that remain hidden in the unconscious (which might account for 95 percent of our true motivations, fears, blind spots, and agendas), we need to bring them into the conscious world so that we can identify them and become accountable for them.

You cannot heal what you do not acknowledge. "Sin" has been the religious word most often used to stand for this hidden, dark, and "disobedient" aspect of our nature. Sin is that part of us that is not truthful; it is any unfaithfulness to our true nature and greatest destiny. In that deepest sense, we are indeed all sinners, and much of the time we act out of that sinfulness. St. Gregory of Nyssa explained that sin is simply our refusal to grow.

When have I experienced moving from one level of consciousness to another? What caused that shift in consciousness?

DAY 32

ERUPTING INTO CONSCIOUSNESS

Most often the only way that the unconscious can erupt into consciousness is through unwanted encounters, painful relationships, and new situations in which we are not in control—most especially experiences of grief, great love, and uncontrollable suffering. These push us forward in consciousness. Nothing less than encounters such as these will force the lid off our guarded identities and reveal to us our real sin.

What has caused eruptions of the
unconscious for me?

Day 33

Educating the Male Soul

I cannot find a single example in male stories where a man comes to enlightenment by taking a course, studying philosophy, becoming ordained, joining a community, or going to school. Those are all quite fine things to do, but in themselves they do not transform us.

In mythological traditions, the young man cannot reach enlightenment until he has sustained some wounds, experienced disappointments, and confronted baffling paradoxes. Like Odysseus, he will invariably find himself trapped between the rock Scylla and the whirlpool Charybdis. This is where wisdom happens.

The young man absolutely must struggle with darkness, failure, and grief. Physically, the darkness can be experienced as pain and handicap. Intellectually, the darkness is experienced by struggling with the riddles, dilemmas, and absurdities of life. There is no linear, clear, or nonstop journey to the Light. Like physical light itself, true light must both include and overcome the darkness (John 1:5), and this cannot merely be done in a person's intellect or will.

What activities have I turned to for gaining enlightenment, and what was the result?

Day 34

Do We Have to Leave the Garden?

In mythology, anywhere we encounter the prohibition, "don't do this," you can be sure that the young man—the hero—will do just that. There are almost no exceptions to this pattern, starting with dear Adam and Eve. That's apparently much of the point of religious law—to be broken and then struggled with (at least that's what, in essence, Paul says in his Letter to the Romans). Only then does the person experience the needed sense of separation, alienation, and loss from the great mystery and from his own truth. Only after that can he long to return to the garden.

And so the negative seems to create and call forth the positive. The fall calls forth the restoration. Being cast out of the garden teaches us how much we long for the garden. Breaking the rules shows us why the rules were there to begin with.

How has the negative called forth the positive
in my life?

Day 35

What We Miss

"Those who are well have no need of a physician, but those who are sick; I have come to call not the righteous but sinners" (Mark 2:17).

It is seemingly necessary to experience alienation and aloneness, the path of the fall, before we even desire the path of the return. Most of us need to feel the separation acutely before we know what we really desire and actually want. We can't enter the garden freely on our own until we've become separated from the garden. The so-called "fall" of Adam and Eve is not something unfortunate that happened; it is a blueprint for what will and probably must happen to each of us.

What it all boils down to is this: one day a man must wake up and realize, "I'm a complete dumb ass, and I'm sick and tired of being sick and tired." Mature spirituality might well begin only at that point.

At what point did I begin to understand what I truly long for, what I miss?

Day 36

Unknowing

Enlightenment (John 8:12) cannot be manufactured, manipulated, or delivered on demand. It is always given from another. Wisdom is not a do-it-yourself project. The Spirit blows where it pleases, and for those of us on the journey, all we can do is listen for the lessons and remain open. Jesus called this faith.

All we can really do is ask for the grace to be open and willing enough to recognize the secret doorways God opens for us. The door is almost always some form of suffering— physical, relational, emotional, intellectual, or structural. I define suffering as what happens to you whenever you are not in control.

Enlightenment is not about knowing as much as it is about unknowing; it is not so much learning as unlearning. It is about surrendering and letting go rather than achieving and possessing. It's more about entering the mystery than arriving at a mental certitude.

Enlightenment is all gratuitous grace, and the only reasonable response is a grateful heart and the acknowledgment that, always, there is more to the mystery.

When have I experienced enlightenment, and what was the impetus?

Day 37

Hitting the Wall

Every heroic journey begins with good fanfare and wild hopes; you need that impetus to get started. In the middle of the journey, however, you begin to hit your limits. In your twenties, it feels good being the hero, putting your ladder against walls and charging ever upward, conquering this and that. By the middle of the story, heroism fails you. Maybe you realize that your ladder is leaning against the wrong wall, as Thomas Merton said. Along the way, you find that you are quite an ordinary man. Maybe to accept that is your real heroism.

This is surely why Jesus' life speaks to those who have hit their limits. He doesn't look like the typical hero but more like a victim, a failure by most standards—railroaded and executed in the prime of his life.

The sad thing is that most cultures praise and reward the early heroism of the first half of life and look the other way when it comes to the quiet holiness and faithfulness of actual saints in the middle of the journey.

What happens to my commitment as I move away
from the beginning of my journey, where all is
bright and hopeful?

Day 38

Tough Love

Youth need to *earn* respect and status from older men, and this is not all bad. In their later years, men gratefully recall their toughest teachers and most demanding bosses and coaches. They know that those were the people who pushed them to be their best.

A man often knows that those were the teachers who took him seriously, the mentors who saw something of worth and value in him. It is a tough love, but it's love nonetheless. And as long as it's not cruel or demeaning, it's a kind of love that a man respects and honors. Love does not work for a man when it is given away too quickly or easily. It turns him into a lazy manipulator instead of a man of character and strength.

It is interesting to me that the Gospels portray Jesus showing both unconditional and conditional love. We need both loves to grow up properly: conditional love when we are strong and brash, and unconditional love when we are weak and self-doubting.

Who were the teachers and mentors who took me seriously and offered me tough love? Who are the young men I might mentor and love during my later years?

Day 39

We Need Conditional Love, Too

We need both unconditional and conditional love if we are going to thrive. If we are lucky, we received a combination of both kinds of love from our parents. Experiencing unconditional love as a child gives us a strong base—a healthy, spacious sense of self. Yet we need to hear the sacred *no*—something to bump up against, something that creates for us situations with limits—or we will never go deep and discover the best in ourselves. We need both a total acceptance and a conditional demand against our natural egocentricity.

At its best, a father's love is *also* conditional because it teaches the son inner discipline, reasonable limits to his own ego, and an experience of his own power and skill in meeting the standards of his father. Without it, we develop the soft and self-accommodating entitlement that characterizes so many of us.

When am I best served by unconditional love?
When am I best served by conditional love?

Day 40

Where Did I Come From?

In traditional tales, the heroes invariably come from noble lineage or are secret orphaned sons of the king—although such knowledge is hidden from them. This intuition is brilliant and correct. We do sense that we somehow come from greatness, or as William Wordsworth would say, "trailing clouds of glory." Glory, even in the Scriptures, names a divine identity as one created by God and bearing God's image and likeness (Genesis 1:26). Each of us is something greater than he or she dares to imagine, something beyond what meets the eye, something "hidden with Christ in God," as Paul says (Colossians 3:3).

This deep intuition provides a necessary direction and urgency to the heroic journey. It guides us to where we first came from (to who we are in God), before we did anything right or wrong to create our own identity. The spiritual journey is about discovering our birthright, our beginning, with the same excitement of an orphan or adopted child looking for his birth parents.

When have I sensed my own glory? What impact does knowledge of my origins have on my actions?

DAY 41

WHAT WILDERNESS KNOWS

Even up to the settling of the Wild West, nearly all mythic stories took place in the wilderness or "wildness." For both men and women through the ages, it was in the wilderness that they discovered the soul. The civilized or domesticated world was of our making; wilderness was God's making—the first and natural cathedral.

But now we have created a society that idealizes civilization and runs away from wilderness. Many people are actually afraid of nature. Not only have we succeeded in taming the wilderness; we have ended up taming the soul.

Yet nature continues to speak to something deep within each of us. Have you ever been transfixed while looking into the eyes of an animal? When an animal looks into our eyes, the sensation is almost numinous. The world beyond the human is somehow communicating something essential to us. Carl Jung said, "When religion stops talking about animals it will be all downhill." Being in wilderness brings us back to our senses, back to our deep selves.

How can I make time, soon, to be with animals,
to be in the wilderness?

Day 42

Earning the Privileges of Manhood

Early cultures did not assume that young men internalized the community values and developed personal discipline on their own. It was expected that these qualities developed only as the result of mentoring and training.

The privileges of manhood were conveyed only to those who had paid their dues. Society had to be sure that young men could be trusted not to abuse their power. The community had to be careful not to encourage and empower selfishness. Then as now, young men tested the system by demanding privileges they had not yet earned. Unfortunately, parents and society in general give in to these demands, rather than teaching young men and testing their character.

There were also clear distinctions between levels of advancement and status. The elders had already earned privileges and didn't need to justify themselves to the younger men. Yet the young men needed processes by which they worked toward maturity and achieved that status they so desired. They often fought the process, but they also respected it. We see, over and over again, that men don't respect anything they get for nothing.

How have I been trained and tested? How do I know that I'm ready to proceed to the next level of privilege and power?

Day 43

Being Accountable

Initiated elders know that *from whom little is demanded, nothing can be expected.* If someone receives a free lunch, it will be forgotten, rejected, or lost just as freely. Like Esau, we will sell our birthright for a bowl of soup (Genesis 25:34).

A young man needs a valued group, a community on which he has claims and that has claims on him. This group will send him away, initiate him, and welcome him back. Without this home base, true initiation is unlikely. The group provides an accountability system that forces the young man out of his heady illusions and into concrete behavior.

The single greatest weakness of many liberal churches is the lack of any real accountability for what they say they believe. Too much is subject to ego whims, individual temperament, and current political correctness. Traditional and conservative groups tend to last and produce results that last. Liberal groups tend to offer necessary critical thinking but are too individualistic to create real community. Something needs to emerge with the best of both.

Do I belong to a group that supports me and always holds me accountable? If not, where might I find such a community?

Day 44

A Father's Job

Boys long for male nurturing. They want their fathers to teach them practical skills for success and survival, and they want their fathers to choose freely to be with them. Young men love shoulder-to-shoulder experiences with another man, preferably their dad. A son wants to capture his father's attention. Some people claim that nothing thrills and secures a child more than to see an immediate smile on the face of his father or mother when he enters the room.

From their mothers, boys want nesting, nurturing, talking, and listening. However, it is the fathers' job to lead them into the outer world and provide the vision, the security, and the confidence that allows them to venture beyond the nest. A young man left to enter the larger world unsupported and unguided by his father's encouragement seems to experience a lifelong, gnawing sadness. You can see the nervous twitch of the mouth and haunted look in the eyes of a man—even an older man—who didn't receive this from his father. They never forget.

Did I experience that support from my father? If not, how can I address the wound that is left?

Day 45

Catching Dad's Love

The relationship between a father and a son is almost too deep for words. It taps into ancient, original longing. A son yearns for his father to give him his male energy. But the son wants to know that he has something to give back to his father, almost as an equal. This is why playing catch can be such a powerful memory—it symbolizes the mutual self-giving between father and son. Mutual self-giving is the basic metaphor for God in much of John's Gospel.

Love for our father is the first experience we have of power and importance in another's life. This love is freely chosen: "Dad chooses to be with me not because he has to but because he really likes me. I must be good!"

The message seems to be that if we matter to our fathers, we will also matter in the larger world, which is also bigger, and other, and outside. Possibly this is why so many people seem to prefer a masculine image of God, even though God is clearly beyond gender.

What healthy father-son memories do I have, if any? What healthy father-son memories can I create for my own son(s)?

Day 46

Getting Ourselves Back to the Garden

Men hate to fail. And yet we have to experience a fall. It is the well hidden pattern that the mystic Julian of Norwich wrote about: "First the fall, and then the recovery from the fall, and both are the mercy of God." The man in all of us who falls and fails, who actually must fall and must fail, is called Adam. The man in all of us who gratefully returns, who always says yes, is called Christ.

We can read the entire Bible as Adam's longing and attempts to return home to the garden, where he was fashioned by God and named *adamah*, which means "dust of the ground" (Genesis 2:7). God's last words to Adam were, "You are dust, and to dust you shall return" (Genesis 3:19). *Adam must lose his fear of being dust, which is to lose the fear of being who he is. Eventually he understands what God can do with dust.* Finally Adam loses his interest in separating, and his fear of falling, and returns to the primal garden.

When I look at the story of my life so far, where is the fall, and where is the return?

Day 47

Finding Yourself in Nature

Abraham, Moses, Job, Jonah, Elijah, and Jesus all had life-changing religious experiences in natural settings, not in man-made buildings or even sacred sites. Rather, the sites became sacred after, and because, they were the locations of life-changing experiences.

A man craves contact with the substantial, the solid, the authentic, and the eternal. We experience awe when we encounter ruins and artifacts, ancient caves and carvings, arrowheads and pottery. Is there a boy who doesn't dream of those things? This is the search for our ancient soul, our uncluttered originality in God—or as the Eastern masters say, "the face you had before you were born." Anything natural or old somehow speaks deeply of that face, whereas plastic, drywall, and steel seldom do.

If that primal encounter does not happen in a man's life, religion will have little ability to broker and guide his journey. All spiritual cognition is really *re-cognition* of an earlier and deeper touch of the divine. Encountering the natural allows us to know what we've always known, but somehow forgot. Religion merely seconds the motion.

How much time have I spent in the natural world? What significant spiritual experiences have I had in nature?

Day 48

Men's Rites of Passage

Men need, and want, what the great religious traditions have promised them: a face-to-face encounter with, and experience of, their own deepest life. D. H. Lawrence said, "The world fears a really new experience more than it fears anything." We can dismiss a new idea, but a new experience changes us, and the ego does not like to change. Mature religion fosters experiences of depth, not just belief in doctrines, which asks almost nothing of us.

This is the purpose of a rite of passage: to create inner experience. Note that they are "rites" or rituals of passage, not lectures of passage. Neither are they sessions for solving problems or getting therapy. Some people want to turn a rite of passage into a psychological experience, but it is meant to be an epiphany of life and a facing of its other side, our own necessary deaths. Ironically, this consideration of death causes the greatest growth spurt of all, which is why it was called "initiation." You finally, truly, begin.

Have I gone through a rite of passage that allowed me to confront life and death? If so, what was it, and how did it affect me?

PART 2
The Male in Culture and Society—God, Power, and Shame

✦ Modern men are cerebral, not instinctual.

✦ Part of men's work is reacquiring our gut instinct for what's authentic and what's inauthentic.

✦ Ours is a radically benevolent God and universe—do we believe this, do we know it to be true?

✦ How do we learn to let God be God?

✦ The best teachers are those who share the journey with us.

✦ How would I feel right now if I truly believed that everything in my life belonged?

✦ Are you willing to ask yourself the hard questions:

~ What am I willing to give up to do the right thing?

~ What am I really here to do?

~ Where do I fit in the changing realities of the world?

~ How do I find meaning in loss?

~ Where is real power found?

~ Why do I feel so bad about so much of my life?

~ How do I build a life when it feels like the world around me is shifting beneath my feet?

Day 49

Experiencing Our Experiences

Most men today, especially overly educated men, exist largely in their heads. We are trying to make sense of it all. As a result, we are often unwilling to actually experience life because we want the purpose and meaning up front, prior to the experience. We suffer from too much desire to control and too little faith to "let go and let God." To really understand something, we need to submit to the experience without always understanding ahead of time what it is that we are about to experience.

The wonderful thing about a sacred story is that it is not driven by the need to control or to explain perfectly. This allows the soul to grow inside the story and move around for many levels of meaning. Remember this: *pure literalism always leads to a decrease in meaning.* Mythology and sacred texts try to lead us and allow us to have the experience for ourselves. Through our experience we discover that encounter is not only possible but desirable. So often we struggle with experiencing our experiences.

How have I moved from simply living in my head
to experiencing life more fully?

Day 50

A Wider Universe

Secular culture has stripped us of a process for accessing the deeper meaning in our lives. Without a functioning story line in which to place our own small story, we get lost in our own insignificance. This is why the perfect response to any male rite of passage is like that of Jesus when he understood, "I am a beloved son!" Without a transcendent connection, each of us is stuck in his own little psyche, struggling to create meaning and produce an identity all by himself. When we inevitably fail at this—because we can't do it alone—we suffer shame and self-defeat. Or we try to pretend that our small universe of country, ethnicity, team, or denomination is actually the center of the world. This can bear dire results.

We need a wider universe in which to realize our own significance and a bigger story in which to find meaning. Not only does a man need to hear that he is beloved, that he is a son, he needs to believe that he is a beloved son "of God."

How has the culture around me affected the way
I've searched for greater meaning? Have I found
meaning in a larger story, and if so,
how did that happen?

DAY 51

GOD FRIENDSHIP

Living merely for reward or in avoidance of punishment has allowed us to become absentee landlords of our own lives. We just muddle through, safe in the promise of a heavenly reward if we do our best. So we go to church on Sunday—we get the reward later and avoid punishment—fire-insurance religion instead of any real freedom or love. God is not now, but always later.

We should have faith for the sake of faith itself: faith that God is God, God is good, and that God is—against all odds—on our side! *God friendship is its own reward now.* If you have it now, you will have it then, and that is called heaven. If you don't have it now, apparently you don't want it very much, and that is hell. But both heaven and hell are first of all *now*, and not delayed rewards or punishments.

Is my faith rooted primarily in punishment and reward, or have I experienced faith for the sake of an ongoing communion with my creator?

Day 52

Gut Instinct and Conscience

"You are a letter of Christ, . . . [written] not on tablets of stone but on tablets of human hearts" (2 Corinthians 3:3).

Generally, men are not taught to trust their gut instincts or even to listen for them. Our religious culture doesn't validate the instinctual self; it relies heavily on the cerebral self or the external law (see Romans 2:15 for further insight here). Those of us brought up to be good church boys learned not only to suppress our instinctual natures but actually to distrust them.

As a result, we have been deprived of a more balanced, nuanced, and interior sense of good and evil—a real conscience. We don't know what's good and what's evil because we've relied almost exclusively on theories or mere external laws. It's time for men to go deeper than the law written on stone, as Paul says above. We need to reacquire "human hearts" for what is real and unreal, for what's good and what's bad.

Was there a time when I trusted my gut? If so,
what difference did that make?

Day 53

God's Justice

Many men believe that God is the angry parent in the sky, a deity defined by retributive justice who will make all things right in the world with vengeful punishment. But God's justice is achieved not by punishment but by the divine initiative we call grace, which enables us to bring about internal balance, harmony, and realignment with what is: God. We call this "restorative justice" instead of the human retributive justice, which we have largely projected onto God. We pulled God down to our petty level.

God "justifies," that is, God validates the creation not by parental punishment from without but by positive enticement and transformation from within. Would God be less loving than a good parent in this world? No, God has to be greater than the greatest love you have ever experienced. This is the profound and primary revelation of the Judeo-Christian Scriptures. If we miss this message, all the rest will be distorted and even destructive.

How have I experienced God's justice in terms of positive enticement and transformation from within? What prevents me from experiencing God in this way?

Day 54

The First Permission

Have you ever met a man who didn't seem comfortable in his own skin? Maybe that person seemed to possess an inexpressible sadness, or was unusually apologetic, or was possibly surly and brittle. Consider the possibility that, as a child, when that person first came into the world, he was not given the first permission—permission to exist.

Many people have never been given this foundational permission—either spoken or unspoken. No one ever held their face, looked into their eyes, and said, "Welcome to the world, dear little one. I'm so happy you're here, that you exist. I love you." This is the essential and irreplaceable role of both a mother and a father.

Did I receive the first permission? How have I given the first permission to others close to me?

DAY 55

MIRRORING

Truly happy people—those who enjoy their freedom and possess a measure of self-confidence—are those who received the first permission, the permission to exist. Somewhere in their early lives, their mother or father or someone very close to them such as a grandparent assured them that the world was a better place because they were in it.

But then we usually need a few more permissions along the way, which is a potential benefit of friendship, companionship, and marriage. Otherwise, we doubt ourselves. It seems we cannot mirror ourselves by ourselves; we must always be mirrored by another. All are preparing us for the final all-accepting mirroring from God.

It is only when we experience that someone on this earth is happy that we exist that we can dare to imagine and allow the unconditional love of a radically benevolent God. How truly sad if we never hand on this primal gift to at least one other person, or if we never receive it ourselves.

Who mirrored the love of a radically benevolent God in my life?

DAY 56

THE PROBLEM WITH NOT BEING GOD

Most of us want to be in charge, or at least in control. When we're honest with ourselves, this creates one of the basic issues we have with God—the problem that God is God and we are not. This is not simply a theological issue, but a personal one as well.

Frankly, it really pisses us off that God is in charge of creation and we are only creatures, especially when so much is unjust, nonsensical, and violent.

Do you ever find yourself secretly wishing that you were in charge? That you could call the shots? I wonder if this is not an absolutely necessary struggle with God, sort of like Jacob daring to wrestle with the Angel of Yahweh "until daybreak" and limping away with sciatica, but with a new name, a blessing, and what he calls a "face to face" encounter (Genesis 32:23–32). Quite a good trade-off!

How much time and energy do I expend wishing I were God, the one in charge of my life?

Day 57

Blow by Blow

Part of the reason we want to be God is that secretly we believe we have all the answers, and the right answers at that. This is not only wrong but also not very smart. Yet God is patient in calling us slowly to ever greater wisdom. Usually God does this by making our self-constructed world fall apart. Our personal salvation project must always show itself to be almost totally wrong; in fact, the refusal to allow this falling apart is what creates legalism in religion.

The pain of things falling apart is what we call suffering, and it is one of God's means to show us that life is always bigger than we imagine it to be. Faith is what sustains us through this suffering, and it allows us to discover that we can survive only by relying on a much greater Source.

God is always drawing us closer, blow by blow, and bit by bit. And most of the time we do not even know it is happening.

When have I experienced my life falling apart?
Did I experience God at that time, and if so, how?

Day 58

What We Do with Our Pain

All great spiritual traditions teach us what to do with our pain. If your religion is not helping you to transmute your pain into something good, then it is junk religion. No wonder Christianity's central symbol is a man in pain, a man who is not destroyed by it but rises from it and moves through it.

Never get rid of the pain too quickly, until you have learned what it has to teach you. Then the resurrection will take care of itself. I promise.

What has my pain taught me?

Day 59

God Likes Me

It's hard for men to accept that God loves them simply because God is Love, but it's even harder for men to believe that God might actually *like* them. We can accept on some level that God might love us, because that is God's job description. But to consider that God might even like us, for the ordinary person that we are, for the pure pleasure of our company—that's just too big a stretch for most of us. God must see something in us that we cannot see in ourselves, which, of course, is the case.

If we can believe that God might actually like us, I would say that this is the beginning of truly mystical and mature Christianity. You also become much happier yourself, because it allows you to begin to like yourself too. After all, God cannot be wrong.

How would it feel to know that God likes me?

Day 60

God Is Not Who We Think God Should Be

We see God philosophically as omnipotent, omnipresent, omniscient, perfect, and infinite. But think about Jesus. If he is the perfect image of the divine (Hebrews 1:3) and the revelation of the invisible God (Colossians 1:15), then how does that square with a powerless man on the cross? Even after two thousand years, it's hard to realize what a revolutionary symbol, revelation, and reality the crucified Jesus is. He said, in effect, "Who you think God is, God *isn't*."

We don't learn this through mere words, or we would have learned it from Scriptures alone. We learn who God is through our own existence. We learn to *know* God, as daring as that sounds, by how God accompanies us in our daily existence. For example, we experience Jesus' deep solidarity with us in our painful encounters and in those of others. We see that he is on the side of the poor, the helpless, and the suffering soldiers on *both* sides of every war. No, God is never who we think God should be.

What have I learned about God
through my own existence?

Day 61

The Truth

Beware of becoming a man who is smug in his beliefs: "I know the truth, so don't bother me with the facts or exceptions." Often, though, we get our truth early in life and don't want any further evidence. This not only shuts us off from grace but also makes us unbearable to live with!

One of the many wonderful things about Jesus is that he never has any trouble with exceptions. He did not insist on perfect order, but found God in the disorder, the sinners, the excluded, and the handicapped. This is definitely a new kind of religion.

How open am I to constantly revising what I believe is the truth? How willing am I to adapt and learn things that change my view of the world?

Day 62

Wanting to Do What We Have to Do

There is a profound difference between living in the addictive society of the modern secular world and living in the liberation of Jesus' teaching. In the addictive culture, many of us just *have to do what we want to do*. We can't help ourselves, and this becomes addiction at many levels; primarily it's an addiction to ourselves.

Those of us who embrace the gospel of Jesus have learned by grace *to actually want to do what we have to do!* What else would freedom be? What else would love be?

Can I discern the difference between having to do what I want to do as opposed to wanting to do what I have to do? How can this shift change my life?

Day 63

Merit and Demerit

A lot of good men were conditioned to see the world inside an equation by which we get what we deserve—no more and no less. If we want something, we've got to work for it. This is stamped on our psyches, the message received from parents, teachers, coaches, priests, Boy Scout leaders, and society in general. I call it "meritocracy." But in that model there is no room for mercy, forgiveness, or the real meaning of God's love.

We have to experience many bumps and falls before we perceive God's love upholding us. Only then can that love interact with and break down our conditioning and allow us to trust love that is unmerited. If we never receive such love, we won't know how to hand it on to others. Surely this is what Jesus meant when he said of the sinful woman, "Her sins, which were many, have been forgiven; hence she has shown great love" (Luke 7:47). Jesus melted away meritocracy from every side, leaving us free to let love flow.

How far have I progressed from the view of getting what I deserve to that of receiving God's unearned love? How able am I to extend that love to others?

Day 64

Completing the Circuit

The first and essential commandment of Jesus is for us to "love the Lord [our] God with all [our] heart, and with all [our] soul, and with all [our] mind, and with all [our] strength" (Mark 12:30). But how could we love, trust, or even like a God who would just repeat the old story line of every base culture—an honor-shame system of merits and demerits? How would we ever feel safe or close to a God who would allow us to lose everything through one false move? Would you call such a person your friend? My lesser friends are even better than that. This is not divine revelation or Good News.

It's only when we experience God's unconditional love for us—immediately and particularly—that we can be free to love God in return. In fact, we are actually completing the circuit, because this is the God we receive, loving God through us and toward others. "You received without payment; give without payment" (Matthew 10:8).

How have I been shaped by the merit and demerit system? What has made it possible for me to accept—or even begin to accept—God's unconditional love for me?

Day 65

The Problem with a Permissive Society

A permissive society refuses to offer a young man the necessary boundaries that provide him with a healthy NO. As a result, immature men have no solid ego structure and no well-rooted sense of identity. They are everywhere and nowhere at the same time. They are entitled, but for no good reason. They develop little or no impulse control, which is necessary for basic socialization and friendship.

Our market-driven culture is interested only in commodities that can be bought and sold, so we ignore any need for the "sacred no" to our acquisitive nature. Our religious institutions, in panicked overreaction, send us lots of "no" messages, but they no longer feel sacred, just moralistic.

Young men need to experience *both a big vision and their own limits*. They need wise elders who can help them become disciples of the One they meet in that space—the One who offers a convincing and penetrating yes to their soul—a yes so deep (2 Corinthians 1:20) that it evokes both their own personal yes and their necessary no as well.

How have I been affected by this permissive society? How has it affected my sons or other young men I know?

Day 66

Misandry

Misandry is hatred toward men, and it is a characteristic of these times. Just being a man, particularly if you are white, educated, or comfortable, is to be set up for criticism. Men are fair game in cartoons, television shows, and circles of popular, political, or academic discussion.

It's important to help both men and women see that masculinity is not the same as patriarchy. Patriarchy, which has merited some of the misandry, is highly degenerated masculinity—maleness at its worst, you might say. Yet a lot of men have never abused power; they don't even have the power to abuse. A lot of women who have acquired power have abused it as badly as some men have.

Some discussions promote the feminine as inherently virtuous and the masculine as inherently evil. As a result, more and more men are feeling very beaten up and insecure. None of us really knows what damage this is doing to boys and young men. Misandry is yet another example of the human inclination toward dualistic and punitive thinking.

How can I be aware of misandry and not allow it to hurt the young men and boys in my circle of influence?

Day 67

THE MAN IN THE MIDDLE

The middle-class man typically comes to religion for the sake of social support and community, or because of his wife and children. In the first half of life he is concerned with climbing the career ladder, obtaining more money and status. He exists in the male world of competition and comparison, and so topics of divine intimacy, relationship for the sake of relationship, love responding to Love for no necessary reason, or even mystery itself does not appeal to him much during this stage. *He is trying to solve all the mysteries, with no thought whatsoever of entering into one!*

It is most likely that the men reading this book are middle-class, probably middle-aged as well. They are working hard to support their families, trying to do well in their chosen careers and to keep a healthy balance between spirituality and daily life. A serious spiritual journey is just not on most men's radar until later in life, and sometimes not even then because the old, overused neural grooves of fight or flight are the only ones left.

What do I truly seek from religion,
from a faith life?

Day 68

The Gospel of the Poor Man

The poor man, the man on the bottom rung of society, comes to religion to meet his survival needs. He comes asking life-and-death questions. He's not very interested in theories and theology. If it isn't real, he won't listen. He wants to know if what we're preaching is what we're living, and if it will help him live, too.

I'm sure this is why Jesus said in his inaugural address that he came "to bring good news to the poor" (Luke 4:18). The poor force us to deal with the soul survival questions that are at the heart of the gospel. The middle and upper classes, even the clergy, have played with the gospel for far too long. It has become an intellectual abstraction and a system by which to maintain social order.

We have to preach to the poor first of all to save ourselves. We need conversion so that we can recognize the most basic spiritual questions, so that we can recover our sense of compassion and inclusivity, so that we can rediscover the heart of God.

Do I look to God for my very survival? How can I make an effort to bring the gospel to my poorest brothers?

Day 69

Codependence

One of the greatest relationship challenges for men and women is codependency. This is love that does not have any grounding and ends up feeding our mutual neediness. It always disappoints, and even deeply so. *Only that which is first separate and to some degree sufficient can also unite and create anything strong or good.* Codependence describes the false meaning of what we call love today. It is mostly "need love," largely incapable of "gift love." No other person, despite all the songs to the contrary, can make you whole or holy. That is always an inside job.

Much of what we call love and loyalty is really fear and insecurity: fear of going on the journey, fear of being alone, fear of asking the real questions, fear of being honest with ourselves. I love to say that the best cure for loneliness is being alone!

If I'm honest, do I see relationships in my life that might be called codependent? If this is true, what help do I need to heal those relationships?

Day 70

Faith as the Freedom Not to Know

Cultural Christianity and today's civil religion define *faith* narrowly and wrongly to mean having certitude about things. Actually, it is exactly the opposite! Biblical faith is the freedom *not* to know, *not* to have answers for everything, to be able to combine a degree of knowing with a degree of not needing to know—because we are being held at a level deeper than cerebral knowing.

So faith is actually having the security to be insecure, enough certitude to entertain a good degree of uncertainty, enough full-body knowing that we don't give the whole job of understanding to our minds alone. This knowing does not need to eliminate all doubt but includes creative doubt in the process—which is why true faith is always humble and receptive to more information.

This can look like arrogance or delusion to those who don't experience it for themselves. Healthy believers are no better than nonbelievers, but they can be happier because they don't need to prove that they're right. Healthy believers are actually less dogmatic than most atheists I know.

How do I experience faith? How do others
react to my faith?

DAY 71

IS GOD IN CHARGE?

We might think that God is totally in charge, when in fact God is very seldom in charge. For most of us, God is in charge maybe a few moments each day. God's constant posture toward us is love, which means that God is purposely out of the control mode. If God were in control, the world would not be in the shape it's in. I'm afraid that God's love patiently allows us to control a lot of what's happening in this world.

God waits for us to reach a point of willingness to participate freely in whatever God is doing. When we willingly give our lives to God and ask for guidance, life begins to fill with all kinds of synchronicities, "coincidences," surprises to everyone but you; this is what the saints call divine providence. God is in control only when we give God control, and that is when the really good things begin to happen. In the meantime, it appears that God does everything God can to influence and heal our misguided events.

In what ways do I reject love and try to be in control? In what ways do I give control back to God?

Day 72

Workaholics for God

Many of the most successful and hardworking men, men with the best of intentions, spend their whole lives as virtual workaholics for God or family. They hope their commitment of energy and investment of time will save their soul, support their family, and make them worthy of eternal life. In this way we seem to avoid the depth and joy of life right now—so that we can get extended life later, which is an odd strategy. Do we really want life, or not?

Meanwhile, God keeps gently breaking in, tapping us on the shoulder, trying to get our attention to let us know that achievement and worthiness were never the issue. The issue was always, and only, about relationship. Brothers, do not avoid relationship with God in favor of supposed good work for God or anybody else. That is precisely what so many sons resent about their fathers: "He made money for the family, but he never just wanted to be with us."

When am I most likely to try to be worthy
of God's kingdom?

Day 73

Shoulder to Shoulder

Men relate to one another better shoulder-to-shoulder than face-to-face, which is the mode women most prefer. Women often experience men as unwilling to talk, lacking in vulnerability, and out of touch with their feelings. Experts hypothesize that women's operative vocabulary for feelings and inner states is probably 5–1 compared to most men. We seem to be falling out of many conversations, some of which are needed and important for right relationship.

Men, however, will stick together in the trenches, on their teams, and with their tasks, feeling a kind of union, loyalty, and caring, a very real bonding with their fellow men in *doing* rather than talking. In active group tasks, men are not usually competitive but literally shoulder-to-shoulder in their work. This is actually *a male style of intimacy*, which women do not always understand or appreciate. It can lead men to great love, hard work, and sacrifice for others. This might explain in part why sports, war, and physical work appeal to men; such shoulder-to-shoulder activity provides a way for them to connect and be in relationship.

What situations do I remember in which
I was shoulder-to-shoulder with others,
intent on a shared task?

Day 74

Woman's Work

We serve a lot of women through our men's materials at www.malespirituality.org, helping them to understand the men in their lives and to find the themes that apply to them as women. I'm always humbled by women's spiritual curiosity and their constant desire to grow. Most events that are religious, volunteer, self-help, book-centered, or social are attended by at least two-thirds women and at best one-third men.

In Western culture, women have been encouraged, and at times forced, to work on their inner lives much more than men have. When you don't have exterior power, you go inside to find your power, and in many cultures this interior power has become a major strength for women. Surely they appear to be more comfortable than men with emotions, tears, touch, social skills, discussion of interior states, and sustenance of relationships. Thus they have a huge head start in understanding spiritual matters. This is why men must do their work before they can begin to catch up, in a sense. We need to develop men and women who can be true partners.

Whom do I know, male or female, who is truly in touch with the inner life?

Day 75

Mother Love

Our mother's gaze is our first relational imprinting; our mother's early mirroring stays with us our whole lives. She sets the first pattern. If there is no one there to take her place, we are "unmirrored" and ungrounded, often not at home in our own body. I am told that the early focusing of a baby's gaze is precisely the distance between the mother's breast and her eyes. I am sure you have seen how mother and child fix on each other with total delight during breastfeeding. It is almost eucharistic.

In fact, for the rest of our lives, we seek that look again; we long to experience someone who takes delight in us. It is the endless look of love that never stops satisfying, and it gives us a jolt of excitement when we perceive someone blessing us with their eyes. It's a shame when this look too easily becomes sexualized because that's not usually what the soul wants. In that look of love, the gift has already been given, if only we can believe it and hold it.

What has been my experience of mother love?

Day 76

Fathers and Sons

The conflict between fathers and sons is not so difficult to understand. A man has a woman's total adoration, and then they have a son together. Almost overnight, and without realizing it, the woman might transfer some of her love from the husband to the son. The husband feels rejected and hurt. The son loves being the center of his mother's world, but eventually he senses that his dad doesn't like him much. The dad in turn feels guilty for resenting his son, but on a level he's not aware of he is in competition with the son. Both are confused. Both are in love with the same woman, and she loves both of them but in different ways.

The boy grows up doing everything he can to please his father, but nothing works. He gets beaten down and wonders, *What can I do to make this guy like me?* or just *What is wrong with me?* Invariably, the son assumes that he is the problem, that he is simply unlikeable. This self-concept becomes the script for his life.

How have I experienced my father's love? How have my children experienced my love?

Day 77

Living with God Hunger

How do we commune with a God we cannot see? We catch a glimpse of God in something or someone and think, *Yes, this is it.* We draw close, but it doesn't last. We lose interest until something again piques our desire.

If we live authentically and stay on our spiritual quest, we will be lonely more times than not. This loneliness is necessary, and it draws us forward on the journey, but none of us are at home with the loneliness. We find it easier to create anything that will fill the hole: moralisms or practices that we think will entice God to return to us. We find means of artificial stimulation, which trick us into thinking that we're satisfied. No one has taught us to trust the longing. As St. John of the Cross said, and I paraphrase, God just waits for vacuums that God can fill. Offer God the vacuum, and refuse to fill it yourself.

We need to learn how to live with God hunger, which provides energy for the journey itself.

---

*When have I encountered God in such a way that
I experienced love? When have I been the most
dissatisfied with my life?*

DAY 78

THE WOUNDS OF PATRIARCHY

As men, we have a lot of work to do. First, we need to recognize the long-term damage that patriarchy—the misuse of male power—has done to us and to the world. It has damaged women, men, children, the planet, and most social systems, which are still based on domination rather than cooperation. I remember asking some Latin American missionaries many years ago what would be the one thing they would change in South America if they could. They all agreed: "machismo"! It underlies most of the corruption found in politics, church, family, and relationships in general. Of course, the church cannot address this because the church is part of the problem.

I am convinced that the reason Jesus chose twelve men to work with was that they needed the most help, and until they changed the power equation, history itself would not change, nor would people change. They were his test and study group! He did not exclude women from the inner circle for being incapable of leadership, which is how church patriarchy has interpreted it.

Whom has patriarchy badly damaged in my life?
In what way was the damage done?

Day 79

From the Inside

Part of the problem for men today is that our religious institutions don't help us access authentic encounters with the holy, or even with our own wholeness. Mainly we get rules and mandates, signposts and appealing images, which are designed to create religious identities and boundaries. All of those things happen outside the self; thus, they do not develop any significant interior life.

True happiness, like true enlightenment, always occurs from the inside out. When we spend too much time on the outside, we tend to stay there, and we substitute forms, rituals, doctrines, and words for any actual experience of grace, mercy, or God.

If I could design a true encounter with the divine, what would it be like?

Day 80

True Religion

Religion often begins in mysticism and ends in politics. It started with Moses, and it leads to Ken Wilber's formulation today, which says that spirituality invariably "starts elitist and ends up egalitarian." The trouble is that so many people stay in the starting place of elitism.

Where have I seen religion turn into politics?

Day 81

Nondual Thinking

In some Native American cultures, a homosexual person was often the shaman, or medicine man, of the community because he combined both the masculine and feminine qualities in one person. In many parts of India the gay person is simply considered a third gender. This is very hard for the Western dualistic mind to process. What does not fit our either-or categories, others see as a different order altogether.

Each of us needs to accept and combine the masculine and feminine aspects of our personality as we grow older, just as we have the capacity to love both genders in very healthy and life-giving ways. Even if Christians would insist that homosexual persons are of a "lower" order, then St. Paul has a binding order for them: "The members of the body that seem to be weaker are indispensable, and those members of the body that we think less honorable we clothe with greater honor, and our less respectable members are treated with greater respect" (1 Corinthians 12:22–23).

How loving and accepting can I be of both the masculine and feminine aspects of my personality?

DAY 82

HOMOSEXUAL AND HETEROSEXUAL MEN

An area in need of healing is between heterosexual and homosexual men. Heterosexual men need to acknowledge and honor the experience of their homosexual brothers. Homosexuals have their own journey to walk, and if they are to be mirrored by any unconditional God love, it is almost certainly to come from another man. Why would we begrudge them that? Or want to send them underground?

Even Jesus was comfortable with another man placing his head on his chest, and the Gospel writers were not afraid to say that, nor was the "beloved disciple" afraid to brag about it.

Same-sex love is not going to go away because dualistic Western civilization or churches do not like it or are unwilling to deal with it. Tolerance is not enough at this point; respect, understanding, and real love of our gay brothers is now needed. It is a matter of justice, human rights, and simple love.

What is my level of comfort, or respect, or acceptance of men whose sexual preference is different from mine?

Day 83

We Fall Short

God fills the gap of human deficiency by a cosmic act of mercy and compassion. St. Paul's word for that great act is *Christ*. For Paul, Christ existed from all eternity and became visible only in Jesus. Christ is God's great compassion, God's great plan, and God's readiness to fill in all the gaps of human sin, brokenness, poverty, and failure. God's plan is not a begrudging mop-up exercise after the fact. Salvation was the plan from the beginning, not a mere response to our mistakes (see the first chapters of both Ephesians and Colossians). Christ was, from the beginning, God's plan for total and final victory. We are saved by grace and God's unconditional love. No exceptions.

So why do we turn the gospel into a cheap worthiness contest? Who, really, is worthy? The pope? Me? You? Why can't we accept that God does not love us because we change? God loves us *so that* we can change. God does not love us because we are good; God loves us because God is good.

How much do I trust God's mercy to take care of my every deficiency and sin?

DAY 84

ON THE BOTTOM

We are much more likely to find the truth at the bottom and the edges of things (i.e., of the social/political/ economic structure) than at the top or the center. People at the top and the center always have too much to prove and too much to protect. Yes, those at the edge and the bottom can become bitter and greedy, too, but often life at the bottom or the edge produces a high level of compassion and a great number of seers.

People on the top are often slow learners spiritually; successful people can be hard-pressed to hear the gospel message. It's the people on the bottom who have a head start toward the truth and toward questions of truth and justice. Jesus began with that very assertion: "Blessed are the poor in spirit" (Matthew 5:3). How did we miss that? Could it be because we like the top more than the truth?

What aspects of my life might keep me from facing the truth?

Day 85

When Faith Gets Real

Eventually a man of conscience must ask himself why there is so much oppression, injustice, and human cruelty in our world. Why is so much of the world hungry? Why are "Christian" countries no better and often worse than other countries in terms of equality, mercy, and justice? This may compel a man to look at the role of multinational corporations, the military-industrial complex, or human sinfulness. Then perhaps an alarm sounds—"This is political talk!"—and he closes down any further inquiry.

The holy Archbishop of Recife, Brazil, Dom Helder Camara, summed it up so well. He said, "When I feed poor people, they call me a saint. When I ask why there are poor people, they call me a communist." I met Dom Helder once, shortly before he died, and he was one of the few people I've ever met who actually appeared to *shine* with joy and peace! He both fed the poor and asked "Why?" and "Does it have to be this way?"

Where has my conscience brought me so far?
What must I face?

Day 86

Inner Authority

In the Catholic tradition, men tend to put their trust in the hierarchy. They will ask, "What does the church say about this?" They forget that *they* are the church. In the Protestant tradition, men look to the Bible for their first and final authority. Both church and Bible are fonts of truth to be respected profoundly, but they are one step removed from the inner testimony of the Spirit. We can't avoid the responsibility of attending to that testimony. Remember, the whole meaning of the "new covenant" first promised by Jeremiah and fully claimed by Jesus and the church was that the law would no longer be external but would be written on the heart (Jeremiah 31:31–34).

It is the Holy Spirit "poured into our hearts" (Romans 5:5) who confers upon people healthy and solid inner authority, and this authority is based on the experience of God's love. Only people of such inner authority ever use outer authority correctly. All others either rebel against it or use it to avoid their own spiritual journey.

Upon what or whom do I place authority,
and why?

Day 87

Loyalty Symbols

All groups hold together around needed loyalty symbols such as the Torah, the Koran, the Book of Mormon, or the Bible. It's amazing to me that each of these groups only barely follows what is written inside their sacred book; often they simply fight and divide over what it means. *It is our identity we are protecting, much more than any eternal truth that we really love.*

What we recognize after a while is that most of the loyalty we feel is to the symbol itself. This is what holds us together mentally and as a group—so we dare not deny that we believe it in our conscious mind. In fact, we assert our beliefs loudly, although our lack of love often reveals the exact opposite.

We can't let the Bible become merely a symbol—a flag we wave to prove to people that we're on the right side. Flags and symbols often get in the way of honest relationships. What's more important is the reality that the symbol actually represents.

What reality does the Bible represent for me?

Day 88

When Truth and Love Suffer

You can't argue with a man who enrolls God in his cause. It puts a stop to all further healthy dialogue. After all, who wants to argue with God?

Such a person assumes that he possesses God and understands God's will *perfectly*, and you don't. Where does such arrogance come from? This attitude occurs too often in overly religious people. They communicate loudly and clearly that they don't need you, or even need to respect you. They already have their answers, and they have found salvation—without you—because they've got God in their pocket. God has now become an *object* rather than the Other in a loving relationship that has the ability to transform the human.

This pattern has given religion in general, and Christianity in particular, a negative image for much of the world, certainly the younger generation. How different from the inclusivity, humility, and compassion of Jesus. Did you ever notice that *Jesus is seldom upset with sinners? Jesus is upset only with people who do not think they are sinners.*

Have I ever tried to use God to further my cause?
If so, what was the result?

DAY 89

THE PROSPERITY GOSPEL

When humans do something good, there's almost always an expectation of something in return, even from God. It's just the way we're programmed. We are hard-wired to seek our own advancement.

This "using" of God and religion for the small self has co-opted the gospel of Jesus in some American churches. It's a pathetic notion referred to as the "prosperity gospel" or sometimes "Cadillac faith," which teaches that if we follow Jesus, good things will come to us in return. Of course, anyone who understands the cross or who reads St. Paul knows that this is the last thing the Gospels ever promise. Any promise of worldly success or prosperity is in absolute denial of the authentic teachings of the Judeo-Christian Scripture.

It has been said that *if you want to tell a lie and get away with it, tell a really big lie that people want to hear—and tell it with passion.* It will usually work.

In what ways have I mentally connected good fortune with God's reward? What do I expect from God in return for my living a good life?

Day 90

Seeking Justice

People who are oppressed or poor know every day that the current system is not just. They have little to lose and everything to gain by seeking justice. People on the top invariably support the status quo. Why wouldn't they? It's working for them. You will always want to "conserve" the system that has got you where you are. Without empathy for those Jesus called "the least of the brothers and sisters," our politics on left or right will reflect self-interest and show little concern for the actual common good.

Starting with the Exodus, and Yahweh's identification with the enslaved Israelites, the Scriptures consistently show a rather clear *bias toward the bottom of society as the necessary starting point.* Any other starting point has far too much to protect and cannot hear or speak what is necessary for the common good.

What has it cost me spiritually to be one of the people on the top?

Day 91

Higher Power

Our suffering today is psychological, relational, and addictive; it is the suffering of people who are comfortable on the outside but oppressed and empty within. This is a crisis of meaninglessness, which leads us to seek meaning in possessions, perks, prestige, and power—all things that lie outside the self. When these things fail to give us meaning, we turn to ingesting food, drink, or drugs, or we become mass consumers to fill the emptiness within.

Bill Wilson and his Alcoholics Anonymous movement have shown us that the only way to stop seeking, needing, or abusing outer power is to find the real power within. The movement's twelve-step program walks us back out of our addictive society. Like all steps toward truth and Spirit, the twelve steps lead us downward, to the power within, which the program rightly refers to as our Higher Power.

How would I describe my Higher Power?

Day 92

Meeting the Real Jesus

Those who have walked the transformative journey through death to resurrection are the ones with the authority to say, "I know God." Theirs is not textbook knowledge but living experience. They have learned to draw upon a life larger than their own. Instead of simply saying, "I believe there is a God," which asks almost nothing of the person, God instead becomes for them an active presence. This is what we mean by the expression, "saved by the death and resurrection of Jesus"!

Mere belief systems create both defensive and offensive people who try to prove "my God is better than your God," which leads to the formulation, "I am better than you."

Jesus, in contrast, *went wherever the pain was, and then led people through it, and finally beyond it.* I believe that this is the very meaning of every one of his healing encounters. Jesus taught people, in effect, how to draw upon the larger Source to make such a passage.

When have I found a need to defend my God?

Day 93

Where Is God?

It is not our place to decide where God is and where God is not. Our great spiritual traditions assert that God is omnipresent. Why do we try to ration out this ubiquitous presence of God? As if we could anyway.

St. Thérèse of Lisieux, an official doctor of the church, found God especially in her imperfections, in her weaknesses and limitations—which she actually delighted in, because they kept her close to God. Thérèse called this spirituality her "little way," but it was nothing more than a long-awaited discovery of the gospel.

For centuries most of mainline Christianity has tried to limit and control the availability of God by using doctrinal and moral screens. We have tried to tell Creator God where God could be and could not be, whom God could love and not love. Thanks to such perversion, many people have felt unworthy of knowing God. An ironic twist, since God only wants to give godself away—always and everywhere!

Where have I seen God lately?

DAY 94

THE HOLE IN THE SOUL

Do you realize how difficult it is for most men—with our fix-and-manage mentality—to surrender ourselves? There's little in our psyche prepared to understand the spiritual wisdom of surrender. It does not come easily.

All the great world religions teach surrender in some form, yet most men don't think surrender is really necessary, until they experience a major hole in the soul—something they cannot understand, fix, change, or control.

Those of us in the developed world—who live comfortably with few apparent needs—must face the limitations within us. We may still have the power to control our money or fix the obvious problems, but we cannot understand, fix, change, or control the world inside us. These matters teach us the importance and necessity of surrender. These are the holes in our soul whereby we break out, and God breaks through.

What are the holes in my soul? What parts of me are poor, oppressed, abused, or forgotten?

DAY 95

SOMETHING NEW AND BIG

The conversion of St. Paul was an inner and authoritative experience. What Paul learned the day of his conversion and in the many years that followed was not textbook knowledge. After his conversion, Paul *knew something*, and it put him at odds with both the Jewish establishment and soon with Peter and the apostles when they gathered in Jerusalem. Paul knew something new and big—on his own.

Every man has to come to the God experience on his own. Conversion is a foundational change of position, perspective, and identity. After authentic conversion, God is not out there anymore. A man no longer looks out at God as a separate identity but looks outward from the God within him. That is what gives him such inner authority. A converted man knows he is participating in something much bigger than himself. Something is being done to him; he knows he is not doing anything himself.

What aspects of my conversion experience
do I remember?

Day 96

Uniquely with God

Probably the most courageous interior thing a man will ever do is trust that his little soul could be in a unique relationship with God, that he reflects a facet of God's glory that no one else will ever reflect in just that way. Such knowledge is not an ego trip; it doesn't make you enamored with your own specialness. It does cause you to fall in love with the God who has chosen you, lives in you, *and loves you exactly as you need to be loved on each stage of your journey.*

If you think this is wishful thinking, listen to St. John of the Cross, a doctor of the church: "God carries each person along a different road, so that you will scarcely find two people following the same path in even half of their journey to God" (*The Living Flame of Love*, 3:59). It makes you wonder why we ever thought that generic law, administered in absolutes, could ever deal with the beautiful complexity of the soul in relationship to its God.

What are some of the qualities of my unique journey with God?

Day 97

How Am I Defined?

Are you defined by people's response to you? If you are, then you've laid down a sandy foundation for your life. You'll find your moods swinging up and down wildly, depending on what everybody thinks. Similarly, defining yourself by how you feel is a moment-by-moment drama. Such an identity is based on narcissistic reactions as opposed to anything true. You will wonder which feelings are your real feelings, and which ones really matter.

Jesus put it this way, and I paraphrase: How can you believe, when you look to one another for approval instead of the approval that comes from the one God? (John 5:44)

This is the burden of the modern self: insubstantial, whimsical, totally codependent, and all the while calling itself "free" and educated. At some point we must identify the meaning of our lives within ourselves, in terms of our radical relatedness to God. As St. Francis put it, "We are who we are in the eyes of God, nothing more and nothing less."

Where do I turn for self-definition?

DAY 98

APART AND SEPARATE

Men in America come from a tradition of rugged individualism. We see ourselves as autonomous individuals. We start from a place of separateness and then desperately try to become part of a community, but we don't know how.

Whereas many poor people take their communities for granted, most men in our world have difficulty even finding a community to call their own. We have lost the ability to operate for the common good as opposed to my private good, and this has made it largely impossible to understand even the basic message of Jesus. *The biblical revelation is God saving history, and not just saving me apart from everybody else.*

If we do not go to heaven together, how could it be heaven? Could you really be perfectly happy for all eternity if you knew that your wife, your children, your mother, the billions of innocent victims of history were not there with you? It would be a false kind of happiness, like being the only guest at the "party of the year."

How have I experienced community?

DAY 99

SECONDING THE MOTION

Prayer is difficult for men because every time we go to church, every time we try to pray, we are trying to reestablish a communion that feels lost to us. Prayer seems like pretend, mere duty, wishful thinking, a pious obligation, or a useless reaching out.

It is a major task for most of us to experience the stream of life that is already flowing through us. God does not answer as a result of our prayer; our very desire to pray means that God is already answering. When it comes to prayer, all we ever do is second the motion. Trust me on that. The move itself always comes from God.

When and where do I relate to prayer
with the most ease?

Day 100

A Balancing Act

It should be no surprise to us that authentic masculinity is the other side of feminine energy. It's the complement, the balance, the counterpoint, the needed energy to create a lovely whole. Together these two energies are always new life and new beauty. Separate they are overstatement, imbalance, sterility, and boredom.

In the Chinese view of the universe, maleness is the *yang*, or masculine principle, that is always the necessary complement to *yin*, the feminine principle. In their togetherness they overcome the dualistic universe, and in honoring each other, they always create a third something, whether it be a child, inspiration, creativity, or just pure happiness. The principle of two always yields to a wonderful "third something." In theological language we call it the Holy Spirit—the Life that flows between the dyad of the Father and the Son.

In what ways have the yin and yang acted together in my life?

Day 101

A Dance of Sacred Relationships

Males are not characterized by exclusively masculine energy, nor do females hold only feminine energy. The new humanity we are pointed toward is whole, integrated, in union, and holy—it's a dance of sacred relationships.

Frankly, one major reason why young men need mentoring by true male elders is that they are either trapped on the male side of things, or they have not even found the male side, which leaves them sort of neuter. Fathers who have found the balance of male and female in themselves are the natural mentors of young men—and young women too. They call forth wholeness in their mentees.

In what way have I connected with the masculine?

Day 102

Engineering Reality

Sadly, a man not in touch with his feminine soul ("anima") is easy to recognize. The movement in his life will always be toward outer things. His head will be his control tower. He will build, explain, use, fix, manipulate, legislate, order, and play with whatever he touches, but he won't touch anything deeply—for he lacks knowledge of the interior of things.

He lacks subtlety, imagination, and the ability to harmonize or live with paradox or mystery. At worst, he will drive machines around in circles, preferably very fast, for most of his life. He is the young man who loves to play video games that shoot, move, or eliminate things, with no risk to the self. Now even older men are doing the same!

A man without his feminine soul will try to engineer his reality instead of live it, much less love it or even see it.

How have I connected with my feminine soul?

DAY 103

HONOR AND RESPECT THE FEMININE

One of the reasons women have become so angry at men is that they're tired of being manipulated, objectified, and devalued. In fact, all of Western civilization is tired of the feminine being devalued. It's tired of the rational "command-and-control" model for reality. For far too long, the negative masculine energy has been running everything.

This is why it's so very important that men do their spiritual work, so we can find the positive meaning of the masculine. One of the first steps is to honor and respect the feminine principle, not just in women, but in all things. Some men, of course, represent the feminine principle better than some women; it's not exclusively tied to gender.

By "the feminine principle" I mean everything vulnerable, interior, powerless, subtle, personal, intimate, and relational. By "the masculine principle" I mean everything clear, rational, linear, ordered, in control, bounded, provable, and hard. Both the feminine and masculine are good, but they must balance each other.

In what ways have I developed respect for the feminine principle?

Day 104

Great Truth Is Always Veiled

Today we know that the right brain controls the left side of the body, and the left brain controls the right side of the body. Science has recently discovered that both sides know reality in different ways. The right knows reality holistically. It looks at context more than text; it does not take things apart but rather puts them together. The left brain prefers analysis as its method of knowing. It analyzes each part, each word. Left brain consciousness tends to create either-or thinking: "If this is true then that can't be true."

One of the major reasons the Bible and most sacred texts have been so distorted and misunderstood, especially in the past five hundred years, is that European and North American minds have become entirely left-brain oriented and cannot deal with the paradox of *both/and*. We impose our definitions of God on reality instead of letting reality reveal God. Frankly, as our very physiology illustrates, we need both hemispheres of the brain to know reality truthfully.

Do I take a more right-brained or
left-brained approach to life?

Day 105

Left and Right

Today's world needs men who have a sense of order (left brain) but who also have a sense of creativity (right brain). When these two aspects can inform and respect each other, we have a whole man. Western society orients us—and especially men—to left-brained thinking. Men who think primarily with their right brain are too creative or chaotic to fit well in our system, just as most modern men would be too "rational" to fit into a primal culture.

We have learned how to move forward with motor skills, but we have not learned how to move forward with our spiritual or psychic skills. We need to listen to reality both ways. Yes, we have to order reality; otherwise we could not read this page. But the left brain by itself is stunted. It isn't creative or life-giving. It isn't the source of inner power or deep meaning. It doesn't make connections very well, and today we need good connectors, because, frankly, there is so much floating data to reconnect.

How can I develop more right-brain function in my life?

Day 106

Church of the Poor

The gospel was first preached primarily to those on the bottom rung of society, and it was preached by men who were, if not on the bottom rung themselves, close to it. It is no accident that Jesus chose ordinary tradesmen, such as fishermen, to be his first followers. He knew they would understand his message, without making it into abstractions or mere systematic theology.

For the first three hundred years of the Christian faith, until Constantine made us the establishment in 313, the church was by and large a church of the poor. How do we as contemporary Christian men stay in touch with a gospel message first preached to poor people by poor people of the first century? This is a crucial question.

If I were truly poor, how would that change the way I think of church and faith?

Day 107

What Owns Me?

In many of the houses of the poor in Africa and Latin America, there are no locks on the doors. In fact, in many houses, there are no doors. In the U.S. we have at least two doors per household and two or three locks per door. Is this a symptom of anything?

As a nation, America is constantly fortifying itself with bigger missiles and better guns. We get upset about health-care for all but see no problem with guns for all. What does this say about our priorities? Christians are often the worst of all in promoting a national security state, while still daring to read the Sermon on the Mount.

It seems that the more we have, the more we want, and the more we fear losing it. Greed and materialism seem to be the fuel that drives our system much more than faith or trust in God.

What do I own? What owns me?

Day 108

The Good News

The gospel proclaimed by Jesus and lived by the early church was concerned not only with the world to come, but also with liberation *in this world now*. The "Good News" that Jesus shared was that people can be free from the oppression, illusion, and death that binds them—*here and now*. We turned the gospel into an innocuous evacuation plan into the next world. If we do not want heaven here, why would we want it later?

Heaven and hell are simply continuations of what we choose, love, and live here and now.

What hopes have I placed in heaven that I could live out right now?

DAY 109

THE ENTRAPMENT OF THE WEALTHY

Jesus' teaching was directed not only to the poor and power-less—the first people to accept and respond to his gospel of liberation—but also to the rich and powerful. Jesus saw the oppressors as being in even greater need because they were trapped by their own self-sufficiency and entitlement (See Luke's "beatitudes" and "woes" for a clear statement of this: 6:20–26). Comfortable people need to be liberated from themselves before they can be liberated for God; actually, this is true of all of us.

The rich are limited by their wealth, the powerful are victimized by their high positions, and the oppressors are oppressed by their domination. They hardly ever see it that way, but I cannot think of a great spiritual teacher who has not said this in some form or another. The things you have, have you. If you have too much, you are really *had!*

How have I been affected by my possessions,
position, and power?

DAY 110

ADDICTION

What are we really talking about when we refer to a culture of "drugs, sex, and rock-and-roll"? Why is it so unhealthy? Because it's about addiction. We're talking about how easy it is for people to regress into the unconscious, which is really nonconsciousness or death. This regression is what drinking and drugs and consumerism are all about. Addiction is not about increased consciousness; it is about decreased consciousness.

Addiction happens when we no longer want to feel our feelings. Addiction happens when we don't want to know our own thoughts or feel our own pain. But you know what? Addiction doesn't work. In the long run, addiction brings *ten times more pain than you would experience by accepting the legitimate pain of being a human being*. Religion needs to be teaching this up front and without apology.

When am I most tempted to avoid feeling my feelings or facing my thoughts?

Day 111

Who Are the Poor?

The gospel sounds very different to a man with a full stomach than it does to a man with an empty stomach. That's why the gospel preached to sated and satisfied people is often grossly misunderstood. They often distort and misuse it for their own ego-centered purposes, for their own control and comfort (although poor people can do that, too).

Still, the gospel has to be preached first of all to poor people (Luke 4:18), sort of like a first-level clearinghouse. They are the only ones who can hear it without attempting to rearrange it for their own purposes. They have a strong "bullshit detector." Their circumstances have initiated them into the essential human paradox: we learn by letting go; we grow by giving up; and words and prayers are not a substitute for action.

Jesus preached to the poor so that they would hear and understand his message and then give it back to those of us who don't know yet that we're poor, too.

What have I experienced of being poor?

Day 112

From the Margins

The gospel is most freely preached from a minority position to a minority position. We don't have to sell out because there's nothing to prove to maintain our position, no lobbies or special interests to please. This is why Christianity always operates best from the marginal and minority position. Or to put it best, *the Holy Spirit works best underground!* Establishment positions have never served the gospel well, although they serve religion well. This is why my spiritual father, St. Francis, wanted us to be "blue-collar" clergy, if we were to be clergy at all.

When you're poor and powerless, the hard sayings of Jesus appear obvious and courageous. For example, poor people will not ignore or write off as a mere metaphor or literary exaggeration the reference to a camel going through the eye of a needle to indicate how hard it is for a rich person to enter heaven. It's strange to me that Bible-based Christians who want to literalize everything never literalize that particular quote!

When have I recognized established religion in seeming opposition to the gospel of Jesus?

DAY 113

SALT AND LEAVEN

Jesus said that his followers should be "the salt of the earth" (Matthew 5:13), but we need to remember that the salt is not the food; it just gives the food good flavor. He also said that we should be the leaven in the bread (Matthew 13:33), but we need to remember that the leaven is not the whole bread; in fact, it is hidden inside, yet still operative all the way through, as Jesus says. We wonder where we ever got the notion of a Christian empire, or that the Supreme Court should enforce our morality. These tactics seem to be at odds with Jesus' methods.

When the church operates as a small community of grounded and committed believers, then it gradually makes a difference in the lives of its members and the world, without getting in bed with power and money. From the minority position of quiet but demanding integrity, we are able to live and proclaim the gospel lifestyle—and that's enough "salt and leaven" to save the world from its own death and self-destruction.

Do I know anyone who is "salty"? What makes this person that way?

Day 114

Outer Power and Inner Power

In the workplace, most men don't have much power. Blue-collar workers do what they are told, which is usually the same thing over and over again. Supervisors and managers have a boss higher up telling them what to do and not do. A salesman is always trying to please his customers. Even top executives have most of their decisions determined by company protocols and policies, by boards of directors, and by market forces beyond their control. We can still enjoy our work and do it with love and integrity. But that's not where to look for our ultimate freedom and power.

Even more sobering is how many of us feel that we have little control over any aspect of our lives. No wonder so many men become passive or angry when they put all their hopes in these external roles, promotions, and performances. The gospel tells us that we must first find our power and freedom within; then we'll know what to do externally. Only then is it possible for a job to become a vocation.

What do I hope to get out of my work? From where do I seek power and freedom?

Day 115

The Rat Race

Our culture deceives men into thinking that they are making decisions, whereas most decisions are made for them. The stress of always meeting someone else's deadlines, of living up to someone else's expectations, and of knowing that another man is ready to step into your job if you perform poorly, makes it necessary regularly to get out of the rat race and de-stress. Thus we always want to get away from what we are doing. *But if you have a sense of personal vocation in what you are doing, you don't need or want to get away from it, because it re-creates you in the doing.*

For a lot of us, work is not re-creative, so we create superficial recreations that do not re-create or restore us. Usually they are mere diversionary or delaying tactics. Life is much the same the day after the rock concert, the TV show, the hockey game, or even the family picnic.

What re-creates me, and what re-creates others through me?

Day 116

Business as Usual

Our present system offers most of us the illusion of power and freedom while holding back any real decision-making power. To support itself, the system must offer illusions of success—promotions, paychecks, and other symbols of prestige—to people who subconsciously know that moving to another niche in the maze is no escape from the totally controlling game they are forced to play.

A larger desk, a private office, a bigger house, a newer car, a more expensive vacation—such are the essentially empty rewards we receive for surrendering our freedom and draining our masculine energy in the service of business as usual. *The only real adventure is the spiritual journey*, which flows from a sense of personal call and leads to a gradual uncovering of your deeper soul, your true self, and a way to serve the world. What else were you born for? Surely not just to pay bills.

How have I experienced the spiritual journey
in the midst of daily life? Or, have I yet
to experience it?

Day 117

Servant Leadership

When a man is prevented from making any real difference in the world, he creates illusions of difference to protect his self-esteem. For some reason, the ego creates and maintains itself by comparison and competition. A man may decide that he doesn't have to do anything great himself; he just needs to know that he's better, higher, stronger, richer, smarter—choose your adjective—than the other guy.

This is a strange and self-defeating model for any positive male growth: "I'm a good man because other men are not as good as me." *Every truly happy man I've ever met has found some way to serve, rather than just being served.* Isn't this what Jesus told us to begin with (John 13:12–17 or Luke 22:27)?

About how many times in a week do
I compare myself to others?

Day 118

Your Kingdom Come/My Kingdom Go

Even when we men recognize that we are being trivial-ized, narcotized, and used by the system, we accept that life has to be this way. We cannot imagine other options; no one has shown us any real alternative.

But there is a way out. We must look elsewhere for our rewards, life, and energy. Of course, we will never have the courage to stop believing the ordinary system until we have something *more* and *better* to take its place. Jesus' name for this bigger picture, a truly alternative universe, is the "reign of God" or the "kingdom of God." It demands that we relinquish lesser kingdoms, and we're afraid to do that because those kingdoms provide the only status and security we've known.

So Jesus offers the soul an utterly new frame of refer-ence *outside* the usual payoffs and perks, and he promises us it is much, much better. We should avoid getting addicted to our smaller kingdoms (Matthew 6:19–20). They pay a low wage and keep us pedaling as fast as we can.

What would my life look like if I loosened my grip
on the usual payoffs and perks?

DAY 119

TWO DEFINITIONS OF FREEDOM

Just because we hear the truth doesn't mean we *really* hear it, understand it, or know what it might ask of us. For example, you cannot liberate anybody until he is convinced that he needs liberation and is ready to pay its price. American crowds automatically applaud whenever politicians speak of "freedom," but nobody knows if their understanding of freedom is formed by American culture or by the gospel message of Jesus.

Freedom *from* restraints and limits is our political understanding of freedom. *Freedom for the good, the true, and the beautiful* is Jesus' understanding of freedom! Ironically, many oppressed peoples do the second freedom quite well, and even better than those of us who have the first freedom. You must know, brothers, these are entirely different meanings to the same word, and many Christians are totally trapped inside the first very limited notion of mere political freedom. Jesus lived in an occupied and oppressed country and was still free, and he told others they could be too.

How have I experienced freedom, and what does that mean to me?

Day 120

The Myth of Both Modernisms

The modernist worldview formed most of us till about 1968, when the "postmodern" worldview emerged to descry the failures and false promises of modernism.

Nurtured in the twentieth century by three hundred years of scientific and social progress, modernism eventually imposed a strong cultural belief in the transformative power of mass education. Tragically, this belief was shattered when two world wars emerged from perhaps the most educated people in the world, the Germans. With genocides and wars mounting through the decades, disillusionment set in—postmodernism's playground—and suddenly the world became a scary place without pattern or predictability.

Faced with this lack of reason and logic, the postmodernist responds that there is no logic, no coherent patterns, nothing but scattered irrational action, and that traditional explanations for anything should be mistrusted—even those of religion. This is the often cynical and groundless world that our children have grown up in. In my opinion, however, the gospel affirms that *both the modernists and the postmodernists are half right!* We need to be both rational and nonrational to access the Big Picture.

How do I balance my own worldview in such hectic and harried times?

Day 121

Unhealthy Climate for Marriage

Too many of us (men and women) are overmothered and underfathered—especially in this age of single moms and absentee dads. This unhealthy culture delivers effects that are lifelong and tragic. Men end up being perennial boys who want to marry doting mothers instead of wives, and women are still looking for fathers instead of peer partners. Soon both the man and woman are disillusioned and think the other has done them wrong. I'm surprised that the divorce rate is only 50 percent.

Overall, we are unready for the hard work and the great adventure of life together. We can create a healthy union only if there was first some healthy apartness. St. Paul was pointing toward the same when he said, "Do not be mismatched with unbelievers" (2 Corinthians 6:14). Many institutions, such as school or church, are re-mothering and re-fathering people who were not nurtured the first time around. "Unparented" people are trying to marry and parent children, and they do not have all the skills.

How has this unhealthy climate affected me?
What am I doing to share what wisdom I have
with the next generation?

DAY 122

FACING THE TEARS OF THINGS

What gives a man substance? He must face up to human pain and suffering, what the Latin poet Virgil called *lacrimae rerum*, "the tears of things." Otherwise, he will remain a lightweight, or what writer John Lee calls "a flying boy," an eternal Peter Pan.

That's an amazing image: an eternally young boy-man forever skimming over the surface of life, untethered, never grounded, without a moral anchor. It is rather easy to do if you grow up comfortable and someone else is always paying the tab. But such a man is dangerous because everything in his life is self-referential and thus self-serving. He lives in a form of foundational unreality. Usually he is unable to connect with anyone else at a significant level. Yet he will be the life of every party—he's fun to be around!—so no one has the courage to tell him that he is immature and superficial.

Until the male is taught to weep, and to empathize with the pain of others, he will most likely remain a flying boy.

What have I cried over? What did I learn from my tears?

Day 123

The Male Spiritual Path in a Nutshell

A young man who cannot cry is a savage, and an old man who cannot laugh is a fool.

This is the essence of the male spiritual journey—in its necessary beginning and its predictable end. If a man can feel human suffering when he is young, he will normally, by some strange chemistry, know how to smile with contentment when he is old.

I am not sure why this is true, but I know it is. This has become our very motto in MALEs (Men as Learners and Elders) in New Mexico.

Where do I place myself on the spiritual journey?

DAY 124

WHO WILL WALK THE WALK?

It's ironic that the people who receive most of the world's adulation are so busy living the unexamined life that they have no time to do authentic soul work. Politicians, actors, athletes, rock stars, the movers and shakers—they don't take the time to walk the interior path. There's little reason to suspect that many of them have confronted their own shadow, which is necessary for spiritual maturity. These are the people who are leading our world—and most of them are men.

We need to become a generation of men who will redeem the name of power, redeem the shape of authority, and redeem the face of wisdom. We at Men as Learners and Elders have taken as our vision to reintroduce the practice of the initiation of men into Western civilization within five generations. We want to be both quite urgent and very modest at the same time.

What authority do I naturally command because
of the interior work I've done?

PART 3
Soul Work for Men—Anger, the Shadow, Initiation, and the Path of Descent

*There is a male way of feeling,
and men need to rediscover it.*
—Richard Rohr

+ One of the gifts of inner work for men is learning to meet the shadow.

+ The shadow is the place we put all the suppressed and repressed parts of our lives.

+ Eventually, in every life, the suppressed and repressed parts of our selves will revolt.

+ The challenge is to acknowledge and honor the shadow but not be tyrannized by it.

+ We are all carrying the wounds of our mothers and fathers.

+ Emotions, like anger, are not right or wrong, they are indicators of what's going on within us.

+ We need to know how we actually feel so that we can find appropriate and healthy ways to express our emotions.

+ Every man is carrying a great sadness within him, which is a necessary solidarity he shares with other men on the spiritual journey.

+ You don't have to fix everything and everybody. You don't have to explain everything.

+ The best ally of God is *what is*.

+ The heart suffers terribly when it refuses to accept *what is*.

+ For men, the way through is down, not up.

+ The way through is the wound, and it's the only way through.

Day 125

Men Are Not Born; They Are Made

From our earliest beginnings until quite recently, men were not born; they were consciously made. Male initiation was the way a boy entered manhood. We've lost this essential rite of passage—and have not provided a healthy or effective substitute.

Eventually the boy must be taken from the female world, the protective world of the mother, and led away by male elders into sacred space, to experience his maleness as something holy, powerful, and wild.

In the various rites of earlier times, a boy was always ritually wounded, tested, and exposed to real limits. Everything pivoted around how he dealt with his wounds. Initiation gave the young man a way to have a respectful confrontation with a much larger world, to break into his own unconscious world, and also the world of nature. Initiation taught the boy that there were more ways to deal with the world than by simply trying to fix, manage, or control life around him. *Initiation taught the male how to bow instead of strut before the Mystery at the heart of all life.*

What can I do to prepare the young men
in my life to encounter the nonrational world
of the Spirit?

DAY 126

INITIATION INTO THE TRUE SELF

Men need a kind of baptism or initiation to set them on a spiritual path. This can take the form of a major failure, an overriding desire, or often a great wounding—physical, emotional, or psychological. We need to fall, to fail, and to jump into the mystery of our own existence, or we literally stay on the surface of life. (Note that this is how Jesus seems to understand baptism in Mark 10:38 and Luke 12:50.) You stay in your small, false self until you are immersed ("baptized") into a larger pool that demands a larger self.

This falling into death and into love (often at the same time!) becomes the necessary journey from the false self to the true self. Without a great defeat, we will attempt to use our ego-self to read and understand what the ego can never understand. Only the true self—who you already are in God—can deal with big questions. Thus, initiation is meant to give you an initial glimpse and confirmation of your true self, or soul. Then the real spiritual journey begins.

Have I experienced a great failure, wounding, or defeat? Have I allowed this to bring me closer to my authentic self?

Day 127

Filling the Father Gap

Along with his mother, the biological or foster father is a boy's first God figure. Humans must build on these initial images of the divine because it is too intense and too great a leap to go straight to God. And yet we also need to go beyond our first images, because God is greater than any human love. *As good as your human father might have been, God is much more so. As weak and unavailable as your human father might have been, God is the healing of that faulty image.*

Without spiritual work, most people will never progress beyond their childhood conditioning, and their childish image of God. Their limited notion of God never moves beyond the negative or even positive image of their own mom and dad. We search out human father figures along the way to help us fill in the gap and make the giant leap into the divine mystery. All biological fathers, foster fathers, godfathers, and father figures are to build a bridge to the God who is always the Perfect Father.

Who has helped me relate to the divine?

DAY 128

FATHER CONFUSION

Most men expect way too much of their father. They want him to be God! Often, they end up disappointed in him. Eventually we have to accept and forgive a "good-enough father." Any negativity gets in the way of fathers helping their sons transition into adulthood. Unfortunately, in today's culture there is seldom anyone else besides the father who is assigned to initiate a son. The godfather role in the church has become ceremonial and empty for the most part.

Among the Navajo, an uncle handles initiation. He's the one who teaches the boy about sexuality and spirituality. He's the one who talks with the boy about pain—as part of life and as part of spirituality. He is close enough to have the boy's respect but not so close that he carries unnecessary baggage. It's difficult for fathers to teach their sons at all, and I am told that if boys are told about sexuality or spirituality at all in our culture, it tends to come from the mother!

What have I expected of my father, and how has that affected our relationship? Who, if anyone, has been available to help me in the transition from boyhood to manhood?

Day 129

Carrying Our Wounds

Without a mythological context or a symbolic universe to reveal the greater meaning and significance of life, we can become trapped in our own small story. And in that limited story, without any larger perspective, our wounds can make us embittered victims.

The Christian way is to embrace our wounds and accept them as the price of the journey. We can choose to carry our wounds with dignity until the time comes when we forget why they were so important or debilitating. The wounds in Jesus' hands, feet, and side are still carried in his resurrected body—this is quite significant! I think we carry our wounds until the end; they do not fully go away but keep us humble, patient, and more open to trust. The healing lies in the fact that our wounds no longer defeat us or cause us to harm ourselves or others. Wounds become our daily offering to God, and they develop in us compassion toward the weakness of others. As my favorite mystic, Julian of Norwich, put it, "our wounds become our honors."

What wounds am I willing to carry from my life into the great sacred story?

Day 130

Bridge Building

Somewhere on our journey we stop trying to explain reality and instead to deeply experience it. This puts us in touch with feelings that we would change our lives for, such as desire, compassion, anger, friendship, loyalty, and love. Such feelings come out of the great unconscious, but they are still largely hidden and confused, and often scary.

We can't risk invading this unconscious land until we've developed a clear sense of identity, an appropriate sense of our own and other's boundaries, and some sense of order and control. This is the task of the first half of life.

Like a bridge across the river between the unconscious and the conscious, our soul mediates and carries the images from one realm to the other. The soul also mediates between the body and the spirit, and builds a bridge to the other side so the conscious and the unconscious can walk back and forth. This is soul work. Opening up this bridge is the task of the second half of life.

Can I describe how my soul has carried images from the great unconscious to my conscious life?

DAY 131

APPROACHING THE GOSPEL FROM THE TOP

Most of us men approach the gospel message *not as it is, but as we are.* For instance, comfortable men with some degree of power tend to see all religion in terms of personal healing and spiritual inspiration. They perhaps feel that something is wrong, that something is missing despite their comfort here, so they come to the gospel with that agenda, never imagining there might be a bigger agenda in God's plan. It is sincere on their part, but also self-serving.

The historical pattern is that they turn the great gospel, almost in its entirety, into a doctrine of inner consolation and personal salvation. There are no social or political implications whatsoever, unless something threatens the status quo. Most everybody and everything else gets left out of such an equation. This is a very private heaven, indeed. This will never end up as the Bible ends with "a new heaven and a new earth" and the New Jerusalem descending to live among humans (Revelation 21:1–3).

How do I approach the gospel? How does my economic position or career status change the way I encounter Scripture and religion?

DAY 132

OUR GOLDEN SHADOW

Men's journey to happiness and wholeness begins when we find the courage to travel deep within ourselves and take responsibility for what we find there—*all of it!* This means a man has to look at himself without flinching, and own up to whatever wreckage he may find. But he also needs to acknowledge and honor the promise, energy, and good life he discovers in the same place. Both will be found, I promise you. Some have called this "the golden shadow"! It looks shadowy, but it is filled with wonderful possibilities too.

What he discovers is that *everything belongs*—the good, the bad, and the ugly. This is hard work, especially coming to terms with the bad and the ugly. It may take a lifetime to realize this clearly and with forgiveness. When we're young men, it certainly doesn't feel like everything belongs, but when we are older, we often know that *it did, and it does.* As C. G. Jung said, "Where we stumble and fall, there we can find pure gold"!

When was the last time I stopped to give thanks for everything and everyone in my life? Have I understood that all of it has meaning, and that all of it belongs?

Day 133

Those Other People

We are all prone to prejudice; we make sweeping judgments about other people—those other people over there—without taking an empathetic look at the possible root causes of people's actions. Our judgments are predictably from our side and perspective.

People who have felt powerlessness, or the pain of oppression or exclusion, form whole subcultures within the dominant culture. Fear, rage, guilt, superstition, compulsive behavior, and hopelessness characterize those subcultures, and those of us outside can seldom understand until we have stood there. Nor can they fully understand us!

Those "other people"—often of another racial, religious, geographic, or socioeconomic group—become a blank screen onto which we can project our own fears, self-doubt, and self-hatred. *Whatever we fear or fail to see within ourselves we will see in other individuals and groups and hate it there instead.* This is one central aspect of the universal scapegoating mechanism, which operates largely unconsciously. This is exactly why Jesus needed to expose it once and for all on the cross.

In what situations have I let prejudice, misunderstanding, and fear sway me into judging others unfairly? Can I look deep into myself to identify the secret prejudices I haven't allowed myself to recognize?

Day 134

THE BROKENNESS OF THE WORLD

Ask yourself if you're the kind of man who keeps at a distance those who are different from you. Do you push the poor to the periphery? Do you marginalize the mentally and physically handicapped? Are you afraid of minorities, refugees, the addicted, homosexuals, prisoners? Is it possible that these could represent what you are most afraid of and deny within yourself?

Are you afraid of not being successful? If you are, poor people may scare you. Are you afraid of losing your home? Then the homeless man you see on the way to work may frighten you—if you even notice him. Do you fear your own handicaps? Then maybe people with disabilities will frighten you. Do mentally impaired people assault your view of a rational world? Do you surround yourself with people who are a lot like you?

Brothers, we separate ourselves from the weakness and brokenness of the world at our own peril. It may be difficult to understand, but separation is a great loss *to* ourselves—and maybe even a loss *of* ourselves.

From whom do I try to remain separate, and why?

Day 135

The First Step

St. Paul said famously: "Three times I appealed to the Lord about this [affliction,] that it would leave me, but he said to me, 'My grace is sufficient for you, for power is made perfect in weakness.' So, I will boast all the more gladly of my weaknesses, so that the power of Christ may dwell in me. Therefore I am content with weaknesses, insults, hardships, persecutions, and calamities for the sake of Christ; for whenever I am weak, then I am strong" (2 Corinthians 12:8–10).

This sounds almost like a testimony at a twelve-step meeting. When the church forgets its own gospel, the Spirit teaches it in new forms. The first of the twelve steps is to admit that you are powerless. It takes a long time to take that first step. It seems that St. Paul made it a whole way of life.

Where does powerlessness show up in my life?
What does it mean to admit that I am powerless?
How is it that God can make me
strong in my weakness?

Day 136

We Can Only Say "It Is Like"

In any discussion of religion, it's helpful to understand that all religious language is metaphor. That doesn't mean that religion is not true or real, but that all we can do when we talk about God or the infinite is say, *"It is like,"* as Jesus did in all his parables about the kingdom ("the kingdom is like . . .").

Heinrich Zimmer said, *"The best things cannot be talked about, and the second best things are almost always misunderstood."* The second best things—such as metaphor, symbol, image, story, myth—are those that point to the first best things. All images of God are metaphors, approximations at best, fingers pointing to the moon. Unfortunately we spend far more time fighting about the fingers than looking at the moon.

Everybody wants the one holy, catholic, apostolic finger pointing to the right moon. So we fight over who has the true finger. Does your finger save, or does mine? Neither of them do. Only God saves us, not our descriptions of God.

How can I talk about something as important as God in my life without getting into trouble or being misunderstood?

Day 137

Life Before Doctrine

It's sad that we've burned people at the stake for choosing inconvenient words or believing unfashionable doctrines. When the object of religion becomes its own language, the wonderful process of transformation it was meant to convey becomes instead mechanistic and controllable. Notice that we've hardly ever burned people at the stake for failing to live the gospel lifestyle of simplicity, nonviolence, and forgiveness.

We presented the mysterious and eternal God of all creation as a reward for understanding God perfectly—as our group presumably does. The biblical God cannot be reduced to an answer in a cosmic exam, but has always been *a living, acting presence that is beyond any words.* This God seems much more concerned about giving you life than giving you doctrines and correct words. If you think I am a heretic, listen to Thomas Aquinas in the original Latin: *"Prius vita quam doctrina"* or "Life itself precedes doctrine" (*De Anima*, II, 37). Jesus made it even clearer: "I came that they may have life, and have it abundantly" (John 10:10).

***What does it mean when I confuse the metaphor
with the real thing?***

Day 138

Glimpses and Hints

How do we come to terms with scriptural texts and religious doctrines? Perhaps the best we can do is touch on those things as living tangents, catch true glimpses of them whenever we can, recognize fleeting notes from their unknown but familiar song, all of which take firm place in the heart. This is why myth, metaphor, poetry, story, art, and song are so important. They are the means by which the mystery and hidden depths of an experience are communicated to us. They never limit meaning by cheap literalism, but often reveal several layers of significance. The early church understood this better than we do today.

For the first 1000 years of the church's history, believers took for granted that there were literal, historical, analogical, symbolic, mystical, moral, inspirational, cosmological, and eschatological levels of interpretation of the Bible text. *Each was true on its own level, but maybe not helpful on the other levels.* Nor did one level trump all the others. This became a living and prayerful experience. Presently, we seem to have gone backward.

If knowing God is possible only by catching glimpses, what in my life gives me the opportunity to catch those glimpses?

Day 139

Judging the Good and the Bad

When we look at the world, we see good people enjoying happy lives, but we also see good people leading very hard lives. More difficult to accept are the bad people who seem to be happy and doing quite well, as Job lamented. Secretly, we may tell ourselves that they can't really be happy despite all evidence to the contrary. Maybe we don't want them to be. We want our full payoffs now, whereas now the payoffs are partial, just enough to grant us peace. I do believe goodness is its own reward, with foundational peace and joy, and that evil is its own punishment, with aimless anxiety and restlessness. But the full resolution seems to wait for eternity.

We demonstrate a small and resentful attitude when we proclaim that atheists, evildoers, and fill-in-the-blank bad people are miserable. We live in the in-between of faith and should never expect perfect logic, retributive justice, or final judgment in this world.

Have I chosen the life I'm living just because it's easy? Or am I living this life to the fullest, for the sake of living fully, for the sake of beauty, truth, and joy?

Day 140

Understanding

When you are overcome by self-doubt and self-criticism, the smallest bit of understanding, smile, or kindness from another person feels like a full-body massage.

Knowing that, let's offer those expressions to others as often as possible.

To whom can I go when I need to counteract my own doubts and criticism?

Day 141

Feelings and Emotions

We should allow feelings and emotions to run their course, teaching us and forming us. No feeling lasts forever. Feelings are not right or wrong; they have no moral meaning. They are merely indicators of what's happening in our lives on other levels. Men who do not feel deeply will not know deeply or act with much integrity. When we are willing to feel our emotions, we are able to access the mystery in our heads and our hearts and our guts. They are a gift from God so we can touch things at a much deeper level.

By not being willing to go into the depths of our feelings, we shortchange ourselves from the great wisdom of the body. By keeping things disconnected from the body, we allow our unresolved feelings to take a deeper and disguised form. Later they come out in other ways—as ulcers, stress, heart attacks, depression, irritability, and misdirected anger—all because we refuse to find an appropriate place to feel and share our emotions.

How do I connect with my own sadness?
Where's the appropriate place for me to
express my emotions?

Day 142

Anger Management

Anger is a telling and necessary emotion long before it is any kind of "sin." The power and intensity of our anger sometimes frightens us so much that we avoid expressing it at all, even when it is genuine and appropriate. Many of us believe that if we don't express our anger, it will simply go away. Others are trapped in habits of constant anger and its manifestations.

There's nothing inherently wrong with anger. You shouldn't get rid of your anger until you understand what you're actually angry about. To understand your anger and what's causing it, you need to own it and work through it. Aimless anger helps no one, least of all the person feeling it.

The New Testament wisely advises us: "Be angry but do not sin; do not let the sun go down on your anger, and do not make room for the devil" (Ephesians 4:26–27). So the inspired author sums it up well: Feel anger, learn what it has to tell you; but do not identify with it, or it will kill you.

How do I deal with my anger? How do I know when I'm becoming angry?

DAY 143

OUR EGO CONTAINER

We have learned how to avoid dealing with too much reality at any given time. We create an *ego container* to get through school, to build a career, and to please our parents, cultural norms, and church. This becomes a necessary outer *persona* ("mask"); it holds what we're comfortable with and what we want to show the world, and eliminates all else.

If you become a "hardened silo," most of your real life remains on the outside, effectively eliminated as wrong, unneeded, or dangerous. The fullness of life, which always includes the dark side of everything, will keep expanding and emerging as you grow older. The ego container must expand to receive more data, more contradictions, more pain, and also much more joy.

Remember that the container is merely a tool to be used. Maintenance of the container is not an end in itself—or we never get to the real contents of our own life, much less the life of God. Our ego container is meant to hold the gift, and the gift is forever expanding.

How would I describe my ego container, the person I show to the world?

Day 144

Protecting the Good Ego

Good parents teach their children early on to have clear and healthy boundaries. Without them, there is never any strong sense of identity. This is the function of early rituals, traditions, laws, customs, and practices. Kids tend to love them, and little boys will fight for the rules; it is only we older folks who tend to overreact against them. Find me a great myth or story where the young man is not defending some sacred trust, meaning, place, god, or cause.

Before we let go of our ego, we need to have one. Before Jesus let go of his body, he walked around in it for thirty-some years. You have to have a self before you can die to yourself. Know that you must keep moving, but you cannot do this until you first have something solid to move! These two distinct tasks of the spiritual life must be kept clear and sequential. So-called conservatives are often better at the identity part, and liberals are often better at the moving part.

What boundaries were good for me
when I was growing up?

Day 145

Heroes and High Towers

The constructing of a healthy ego container is the beginning of the hero's journey. However, once the container is built, there is the danger that the hero will see the container as the contents. He's come to believe that the outer person he presents to the world is the sum total of who he is.

If the man overidentifies with his ego container, or persona, he might spend the rest of his life defending the container he's spent so long building. You see this in men who, late in life, are still working on issues such as self-image and security. They've built a container so high that it's now a tower, and they've forgotten how to get back down and walk on the muddy earth where the rest of us live.

Have I become so identified with the outer person that I've forgotten to continue on the inward journey? If so, how do I get back on track?

Day 146

The Male Way of Feeling

We live in a time when the power of the feminine is rising. This is a necessary and important balancing of the scales. Our health as men and women depends on healing much that centuries of patriarchy have damaged.

But men need to be aware that, during the past few decades, women have been carrying much of the *feeling world* for the whole family. Our mothers, not our fathers, taught us how to feel. There's nothing wrong with that, but we have much to gain from learning the male way of feeling as well.

Men need to rediscover and accept, not deny and repress, their own range of feelings. At its best, my male emotion comes in *calm, collected, and considered* feelings, sometimes feelings that are expressed only at the end of a volatile exchange of depth and discernment. To witness such a beautiful balance, such emotional control, is to know that such a way of feeling is possible, and that it is both masculine and healthy.

In what way do I connect with the feeling world?

Day 147
What Is

The best ally of God is what is—not what should be, what could be, or what needs to be. God and grace can always work with the real; it's the unreal, the fabricated, the illusory that God cannot build on. There's nothing there!

And the "real" is always a mixed blessing, partially light and partially dark, no matter if it's your family and friends, the groups and institutions you belong to, or yourself. The problem is not "out there": your parents didn't love you enough, your spouse isn't the right person for you, your boss doesn't appreciate you.

Start with yourself. You're not perfect, and that's all right. You don't have to fix everything and everybody, and you don't have to explain everything or everybody. Let the perfect God love the imperfect you. There is no other kind for God to love! Begin there, and see where the next step takes you.

How can I better focus on what is rather than on all the shoulds, coulds, and woulds?

Day 148

Uncommon Spiritual Sense

Either we align ourselves with reality and prepare to be let down, or we block out the always muddy real world and bring on so much more suffering in the long run.

This is spiritual common sense, which unfortunately is not so common.

What is my reality, right now?

DAY 149

SOUL AND BODY

Men tend to know their inner goodness and find their inner imagination from their relationship with the feminine. The loving gaze of a mother can help lead a man to his soul, as can that first serious girlfriend, or a wife or partner, or even another man who has met his own feminine soul.

Our soul and romantic body might be called forth by the opposite sex, but very often our physical and external body is tested and validated by an endless world of comparison, competition, and contest of any form. If we do not recognize this, we might well find ourselves either falsely defeated or falsely victorious. We might be giving far too much power to the divisions of gender. In the end, we submit that it is God who gives us our soul and names our body as created in his image (Genesis 1:26).

Where have I found support in the feminine?
Verification from the masculine?

DAY 150

THE FEMININE FACE OF GOD

It's no accident that the more macho and patriarchal a Catholic culture is, the more you will find Mary as an object of worship. I once counted eleven major images of Mary in one church. Jesus was hardly in sight.

No wonder Protestants thought we had made Mary into God. It was poor theology, but marvelous psychology. The soul will find the images it needs to convey unconditional love, and so we Catholics put "Our Blessed Mother" all over the place. She did lead to faith in God many people who had been wounded by men. She still is the feminine mediator for many who have never experienced male love as safe and kind.

It's difficult for men to entrust themselves to a God who is exclusively imaged as male. He will presumably judge them and find them wanting. I asked some Protestant ministers how they got along without any feminine face for God, and one quickly spoke up: "We just painted our Sunday School Jesus with a pretty face, blond hair, and blue eyes!"

Where have I found the feminine face of God?

DAY 151

THE WOMANLY SIDE OF GOD

Many statues of Mary show her with outstretched arms and a smile. A lot of men can remember an image of mother waiting for them when they were little boys coming home from school. Her welcome communicated, "Come home, son, I'll take care of you."

We can have all the orthodox theologies we want in our heads, but deeper down and in the end the instinctual self will have its say. The soul will find a way to break through to divine mercy and acceptance. For many people, the womanly side of God is the only part they understand or to which they can respond. How wonderful that, although Jesus clearly had a masculine body, he surely had a very feminine soul. He was not macho, domineering, or patriarchal by any cultural definition. Thank God, or many of us would never have found a God we could surrender to with trust and abandon.

If I have known God as primarily masculine, what has my soul missed as a result? If I have known both a feminine and masculine face of God, what impact has that had on my spiritual journey?

Day 152

The Sacred Marriage

We have grown up with a patriarchal religion that emphasized law, structure, organization, obedience, group, and loyalty. These are commendable virtues, but they tell only half the story. We've come to the point in human consciousness where we are ready for the sacred marriage of the mature feminine and the mature masculine. The mature feminine would honor compassion, mercy, exception, holy disorder, forgiveness, and healing to balance out the more masculine qualities.

Our job is to find what is true in both. We need to mend this tragic breach between the masculine and the feminine. If we had developed a stronger feminine soul as a church and as a culture, we would never have plundered this planet, killed millions in wars, abused and raped so many innocents, excluded so many from our definitions of salvation, tolerated health care only for the few, or engendered so many evil dictators, as we have during the recent centuries. Christian nations would have been known for healing and reconciliation instead of war and greed.

What would a more mother-centered religion look
and feel like to me?

Day 153

The Great Spirit

We don't have to look far to see models of sacred marriage between feminine and masculine. Native peoples of North America achieved a beautiful balance; their prime deity, the Great Spirit, was thought of as masculine but was also nurturing, respectful, and loving toward the earth.

When Pope John Paul II came to Phoenix, Arizona, to address our Native peoples, he stated that there was nothing in the religions of North American Native Indians that was not compatible with Christianity. He said that the Native peoples already saw the Great Spirit in all things, and most mainline Christians did not.

The early peoples of North America, by and large, achieved a high level of spirituality, not based on the ritual killing of animals or people, or on abuse and destruction in any form, but on enhancement, harmonization, and union in the great circle of life. All creatures were to be reverenced and respected. We have much to learn from others, and much to unlearn within ourselves.

How can the natural world enhance
my vision of God?

Day 154

Longing for the Eternal Feminine

Men often sense a deep longing for something that is difficult to articulate. It's like a memory that won't leave, and it's tied up with our mothers and, through them, to the eternal feminine. It is a longing for wholeness, for God, and for the self, all at the same time. With each loving relationship we experience with a well-integrated woman or man, we understand the eternal feminine a little better.

What is this feeling like? It's as if we have lost our twin and are divided from something that is essential to our very identity. A man might spend the rest of his life seeking that lost part of himself, either consciously or unconsciously.

For many of us, the lost part causes lifelong restlessness and personal imbalance.

*When have I sensed a great part of myself
missing? What did I do?*

Day 155

Wholeness and Holiness

This search for our lost twin, for this missing other, can make us strangers to ourselves. We feel as if we can't find ourselves except through the other. Yet this wholeness finally must be found *within ourselves*, and not by endless romances, flirtations, or sexual dalliances.

Our original identity in God, in which there is no male or female (Galatians 3:28), is our primal union between the sacred feminine and sacred masculine—which is why all sexuality feels like a longing for this lost twin, for the beloved, for the "not me." Remember the very word *sex* comes from the Latin verb, *secare*, which means to cut through or to cut in half. Celibacy is supposed to be a sign that such inner wholeness is possible and good. An unhappy or neurotic celibate undoes and disproves that message.

This search for the other is, of course, our very yearning for union with God. This is why we dare not close it down in the name of some false purity, autonomy, or fear.

How would I describe my own yearning for God?
Does it have any bodily component?

Day 156

The Mutual Gaze

In our quieter moments, we might ask ourselves, "What is this face and gaze I'm always searching for? Who is this other I'm always waiting for? What do I see in the world around me that reminds me of her or of him?"

What if these questions are the only ones we need to pursue? What if our longing for a perfect lover is where we find the energy for the spiritual quest? (Read 2 Corinthians 3:18 in this regard.)

Mystical Christianity has given the soul an image of the beloved, and God as the Divine Lover, because we normally need faces to fall into. We cannot fall in love with concepts, forces, and ideas. Jesus became for us that safe, beautiful, and receiving gaze of God.

Where have I received the image as a beloved?
Where have I seen the gaze of the Lover?

Day 157

What We Are Not Yet

The ache we feel of having lost our twin, of feeling divided and not whole, is what keeps our quest alive. We must keep searching for the other half, discovering it here and there in the world, and falling in love with it when we do find it—in persons, nature, animals, events, and prayer. But we cannot stop there.

We also have to find a way to allow, and to forgive, the ongoing cycle of both fulfillment and loss that will always be there. Every lover will partially disappoint you and yet also reveal to you. Be grateful for both. Nothing on this earth is fully God.

We hope that by the second half of life we come to understand that we're always falling in love with what we have not yet become. Psychologically speaking, this is the withdrawing of all idealizations and infatuations that allows us to find increasing fullness within ourselves. Spiritually speaking, it is pure and simple maturity and holiness.

How do I handle the tension between fulfillment and loss? What's an example?

Day 158

Black and White

Racism remains one of the most grievous problems of our time, which makes it difficult to use the terms *white* and *black* for good and evil. However, they are consistent terms in ancient mythology, and we have to ask why. Blackness symbolizes night, a time when things are hidden and not seen; it represents the shadow world in which there is no consciousness, light, or vision. It has nothing to do with race.

Yet people of color have suffered throughout history because of this symbolism. The darker a person's skin, the easier it seems to be for us to project the unworthy part of ourselves onto that person. This is not logical but is archetypal imagery, and shades of darkness are evaluated even in African nations to this day.

The majority of us with white skin are oblivious to our structured superiority, and we don't realize how skewed the system is in our favor. We are most in need of liberation according to the Gospel. We must take the lead in deconstructing this racist system from the top down.

Looking back over my week, where can I see the racism that was operating?

Day 159

White Man's Burden

The challenge for all "white" and advantaged men is to be willing to go back down to the bottom and try to stand in another man's shoes. We can change the system of white privilege only from within, because we hold most of the cards in the game. It's up to us to let go of the power, prestige, and perks that a self-serving system has granted to us too easily.

In remembering all the hardworking people in this world who struggle to have what we're given, let's not fall for the illusion that we deserve our wealth because we worked harder. We now live in an artificial system in which you don't even have to do any socially significant work to succeed; your money makes money for you by simply rearranging papers and deposits.

The poor world needs liberation from the outer social structures that hold it back, and the overdeveloped world needs liberation from the inner illusions that keep it from seeing the larger truth and the common good.

How have I benefited from an unjust system?

Day 160

What Is Truth?

You cannot be a man who says he loves Jesus and does not also love the truth. If you love Jesus, then you will also love what he loves (John 8:32).

When you seek the truth, you'll recognize it by its unrelenting demand that you surrender your always smaller self. Josef Pieper, by no means a liberal Christian scholar, said that the primary arena for truth is in the world of "interpersonal relationships." Truth is not some Platonic, doctrinal orthodoxy that only a few intellectuals ever attain. *For Christians, "the Word became flesh" (John 1:14), and it is in the flesh that we find both truth and Jesus.*

You can tell when you have met a great Christian man, because he is willing to sacrifice himself and jettison personal and cultural prejudices for the sake of the truth of his brothers and sisters.

What is my most recent encounter with this kind of actual truth?

Day 161

Know Your Filters

As trite as it sounds, a good man has to know himself before he can live an authentic life. For sure, we should never talk about the spiritual life, or about God, until we know precisely how we hear things. What are my biases? What's my conditioning? Do I have an agenda? What are some of my fears and ambitions? *Without knowing how you receive daily messages, you do not have even a basic capacity for "truth." Your truth will be all about you!*

Men who don't know themselves are for the most part incapable of knowing God. Their concept of God will be primarily a projection of their own ego needs, their infantile religious conditioning, and what they want God to be rather than who God really is.

We pay a major price for such false gods. When the real God inevitably fails to satisfy our ego needs and expectations, we will consciously or unconsciously reject God.

How have I projected my own ego and needs onto my perception of God?

Day 162

The Ultimate Act of Courage

It is the ultimate act of courage and humility to accept that my mistakes are necessary and even used by God. Why are we so afraid of being wrong? *There's nothing so terribly wrong with being wrong. Did Jesus ever say, "This is my commandment: always be right"?* Human failure and rebellion are at the heart of biblical revelation. It's sad that, according to a twentieth-century Roman Catholic definition of sanctity—the measure by which we canonize a saint—probably no one in the Bible would make it through the canonization process, maybe not even Jesus.

The sacred texts reveal real tensions and real problems and real people—just like life itself. They don't sanitize the story. We have distorted and forgotten the scriptural meaning of sanctity; the Bible reveals foolish and broken people who make every kind of mistake but still somehow trust God and are used by God!

When am I least likely to trust
my own experience?

Day 163

The Real Revolution

Did you ever meet a man, learn his story, hear how hard his life has been, hear about his sinfulness, and yet realize that he's five times a better person than you are? It seems there's no logic, order, or fairness to human life. Despite the political promises of equality and justice that arose from the French and American revolutions, there is no real equality or justice in the world. That's because the real revolution (*revolvere*, to roll back) has yet to be won: the gospel revolution, which turns most of our cultural notions on their heads.

Two thousand years after Jesus lived here, Christians still have a hard time accepting his upside-down world, in which we are expected to work for justice on behalf of others but not to demand or expect it for ourselves (Matthew 5:6,10–12). This is one of the hardest challenges of Jesus' message. It demands an expanded heart and mind. I'm still not sure if heart or mind comes first, but eventually they both are needed to live such illogical logic.

How has the gospel revolution touched
my life so far?

Day 164

Incorporating Imperfection

There is always one clear imperfection woven into the pattern of traditional Navajo rugs. And interestingly enough, this is precisely where the Spirit moves in and out of the rug! The Native mind and the Eastern mind (which Jesus would have developed in his Jewish culture) understand perfection in precisely that way. The Eastern mind is more comfortable with paradox, mystery, and nondual thinking than the Western mind—and Western languages, which have been formed largely by Greek notions of logic. Jesus did not speak Greek, but Aramaic, which is more subtle, diffused, and nuanced.

Perfection in this mind is not the elimination of imperfection. *Divine perfection is, in fact, the ability to recognize, forgive, and include imperfection*—just as God does with all of us. True perfection is not the exclusion of imperfection but precisely the recognition and inclusion of it! That could change your whole life. The gift of nondual thinking and seeing, or contemplation, is the radical grace that grounds all holy seeing and doing.

In what ways am I still dependent on perfection?

Day 165

Love Is a Decision

Jesus *commanded* us to love (John 13:34; 15:12). Thus we know that love is not a feeling, because we cannot command people to feel one way or another. Love is much more substantial and long lasting than an emotion. Love is a decision.

Jesus did not say, "When you get healed, love; when you grow up, love; when you feel loving, love; when you get it together, love; when you have dealt with all the wounds of your mother, father, husband, or children, love." No, the commandment for all of us is to love now. It is an hour-by-hour decision.

What healing or resolution am I waiting for
before I can wholeheartedly love?

Day 166

On the Other Side of Questions

Birth pangs is an apt metaphor Jesus used for something painful that would bring about something better (Mark 13:8). If we want to bring something good to birth, there will be pain. In many myths, male gods create with a flick of their creative finger. But female gods often create through the pain of labor.

Men usually hope that they can avoid birth pangs by making an end run around them. Maybe that's why we're unable to hear a lot of Jesus' teaching about transformation. If we had an image of God as a great mother who is always giving birth, I think a lot more preachers and teachers would have talked about birth pangs. They would have understood transformational suffering. At least many of us, particularly Catholics and Orthodox Christians, have retained the image of Mary as the sorrowful mother at the foot of the cross (John 19:25) or with the pierced heart (Luke 2:35). Any woman who has given birth understands something a man will never quite get: there is a necessary connection between pain and new life.

How have I experienced birth pangs when new
qualities and wisdom have come into my life?

Day 167

The Gift of Guilt

Here are steps 4–6 of the twelve steps of Alcoholics Anonymous:

+ Make a searching and fearless moral inventory of ourselves
+ Admit to God, to ourselves, and to another human being the exact nature of our wrongs
+ Be entirely ready to have God remove all of these defects of character

The story of the woman caught in adultery (John 8:3–11) is a perfect example of Jesus following several of these steps. He gives the woman a transformative and needed gift of guilt but does not paralyze her with shame. After dismissing her opponents, he says, "I do not condemn you" (shaming people never helps) and "Go and sin no more" (take ownership of your own life and, when necessary, change it).

The other amazing thing is that Jesus stands up to the scribes and Pharisees who want only to impose laws—but exclusively against the woman. He seems to be saying, "Come on, boys, what about the man?" The guilty man needs to do a fearless moral inventory—as do the scribes and Pharisees.

What guilt do I need to own before
I can be transformed?

DAY 168

MIRRORS

If we are to see as Jesus sees, first we must become mirrors. This means that we receive things exactly as they are, without distorting them to our liking or disliking. Then our love can be authentic.

To love demands a major transformation of consciousness, a transformation that has been the goal of all religious founders, saints, mystics, and gurus since we began to talk about love. We must be liberated from ourselves and get out of the way. When your own admired image is in the way you cannot mirror anyone else.

We need to be saved from the tyranny of our own judgments, opinions, and feelings about everything—the "undisciplined squads of emotions" that T. S. Eliot criticizes in his *Four Quartets*. Those judgments and opinions fog the mirror and keep us from seeing clearly. If we do not detach from ourselves in this way and become clear, open mirrors, we don't have any authentic emotions at all. They have us.

What judgments and opinions fog and distort my
mirror?

Day 169

Solitude

Do you know the antidote for deep loneliness? Solitude. Yes, it's true. In solitude, we are able to let reality—God—define us from the inside out. When we look outside ourselves for help or answers, we seek one diversion after another. But when we stop looking outside for diversions, entertainment, or shallow satisfaction, the truest answers emerge.

In solitude we learn slowly to live face-to-face with a Presence that asks nothing of us but presence in return. When we become present to Presence, we experience the genuine birth of the soul. If we've never lived in the realm of pure Presence, at first we don't know how to breathe there. But eventually we allow ourselves to be defined by relationship itself instead of by the good or bad—or even the holy—things we've done. And it is relationship with everything: the rocks at our feet, the air that we breathe consciously, the little animals and birds, the God who is now obvious and praiseworthy in all things. Solitude can connect us to everything else.

How do I feel when I first experience solitude?
What discomfort or what relief?

DAY 170

FIRST WE FALL

The journey around the edges of our sin leads us to long for a deeper life at the center of ourselves. Shocking, isn't it? I am not sure there is any other way.

Ruthless ambition can lead a man to the very failure and emptiness that is conversion. So, is his ambition good or is it evil? Do we really have to sin if we are to know salvation? In some ways, they are correlative terms. Darkness leads us to admire and make room for the light, and the closer we get to the light, the more the darkness becomes apparent.

That does not mean that we should set out intentionally to sin, but it does mean that we tend to see the full pattern and know grace and mercy only after the fact. Blessed Julian of Norwich put it perfectly when she said, "First we fall and later we recover from the fall—and both are the Mercy of God." God allows us in and then leads us out too.

Am I willing to live fully—even if that means failure—to recognize a deeper and truer life? Can I look back on mistakes, failures, and sins and see God's mercy at work even in those situations?

Day 171

What Is Sacred and What Is Pagan?

Several of the early pagan holidays later became Christian feast days. Such days were called "thin times"—shadow times, threshold space—in which God and mystery could be grasped in the interplay between darkness and light. The space between heaven and earth was "thinnest" at this time, as it were. All Saints' Day and All Souls' Day in early November, along with Candlemas in early February, were the major thin times. They occurred approximately halfway between the solstices and the equinoxes. We welcomed those from the other worlds on November 1–2 to accompany us through the coming dark winter. We blessed candles or watched groundhogs on February 1–2 as promises and omens of a coming light.

We must use these shadow times, these thin times, to rediscover and accept our deepest nature as a mixture of darkness and light. *Remember, nothing is secular or pagan unless it is superficial.* When we go to the depths of anything, we discover the sacred and the holy, which we now call Christian.

In what rituals do I experience the deeper truth of the sacred and the holy?

Day 172

Good Desire

Most men don't know what they truly desire. For a lot of us "desire" was a bad word, usually meaning something sexual, surely nothing that would lead us to God. The biblical word we translated as "concupiscence" or "covetousness" was precisely meant to denote bad or unhealthy desires, which was to distinguish it from good desire. Maybe *holy longing* would be the best term now for positive desire.

So the task of spiritual directors is to help men find their deepest heart's desire, and to convince them that they can, and must, follow it. What we desire enough, we are likely to get, because God plants within us the desire for what God wants to give us. Did you know that? The important thing is to wait and listen for your deepest heart's desire. What we desire shapes what we will become, and who we are at the deepest levels. *"God yearns jealously for the spirit that he has made to dwell in us"* (James 4:5) is one of my favorite, but often unknown, passages of Scripture.

Am I still afraid to listen to my deepest desire?
Am I still afraid it will just be sex?

DAY 173

THE LABYRINTHINE WAYS

Western civilization has indoctrinated us with the myth of progress, which basically tells the little boy that the goal of life is to get from here to there as quickly as possible, in lines as straight as possible. The rational mind prefers to see life as a straight, ever-ascending line; in reality, it's far more like a spiral or labyrinth. Christianity once understood this; for centuries, believers would come early to Mass to walk a labyrinth before they dared to celebrate the holy mysteries. Many of the labyrinths were removed as the church succumbed to rationalism. If you visit Chartres Cathedral in France, you'll still find the labyrinth directly before the altar. The Enlightenment-formed Catholics now cover it with folding chairs!

Spiritual progress is typically three steps forward and then perhaps two steps back. This challenges a man to keep his eye on the spiritual path and to learn from the path itself. He might find that the steps backward have as much to teach him as the steps forward—maybe even more.

How do I feel about going two steps forward and
three steps back?

Day 174

Not Preferring but Allowing

Once we begin to contemplate, we see how much our inner chatter and dispositions shape our view of life. These dispositions determine what we see and don't see. They determine what we pay attention to and what we miss; also, what we want and what we don't want. In the I-centered ego world, we are constantly choosing and preferring—and therefore constantly irritated because life seldom works out just that way.

We tend to see things through the egocentric agenda—"Will this inconvenience me?" or "How will this make me feel?" But when the ego leads, we cannot see accurately. We will not allow each thing to be what it is, no more and no less.

The soul, however, does not insist on its preferences. It simply allows. It teaches us to wait, in love. As St. John of the Cross said, "God refuses to be known except by love." In prayer, we always see things in a new light—that first allows, and then sees.

Where does contemplation happen in my life?

Day 175

The Divine Mirror

To some degree, we are victims of other people's mirroring. We blindly accept the evaluations of mothers, fathers, coaches, ministers, and friends as if they represent reality. Even on their best days, others cannot mirror to us our best selves; this is God's work.

When we're assaulted by negative and limiting voices, few of us are strong enough to stand against them. Some of us rebel, but this forms us in a negative way. We internalize others' voices, positively or negatively, until *a larger and truer mirror comes along that we can believe*. This is difficult if the earlier image has become habitual. Giving up that internal habit is at the core of healing.

Until we are grounded in a transcendent reference point, we are subject to others' evaluation of us. The deep affirmation and total validation that the soul desires can come only from nakedness before God, who is *the Mirror that always sees and loves his Son in us—until we can see it too*. (Don't believe me? See Romans 8:29, 2 Corinthians 3:18, or Colossians 3:10–11.)

What voices have most mirrored and shaped me?
Where can I go for God's mirroring?

Day 176
The Grid

Humanity, modern and postmodern, has fabricated a grid, or filter, to screen out anything that troubles our consciences or pushes us outside our cultural comfort zones. Some call it "political correctness" on the Left and "religious correctness" on the Right. Psychologists tell us this is necessary for our survival. We learn to let in certain information and exclude all bothersome information.

Humans have always had the capacity to deny things we cannot or do not want to deal with. I am sure God is patient with that. Unfortunately, the ego self, which Paul called "the flesh," is using this to maximum advantage, but with great loss of soul and wisdom and basic honesty.

Our grid is effectively keeping out much of what Jesus or any great wisdom teaches. Wisdom is just too counterintuitive, and too destabilizing for the imperial ego.

What kind of information am I most likely
to filter out?

Day 177

Love as the Proof

No man in God's world is built up by tearing another person down; such behavior insults God, you, and the other. You can't be for God while you hate other humans. John says that if you do, you are a "liar" (1 John 4:20)! Yet it is amazing how bigotry, hatred, torture, prejudice, killing, excommunication, and shunning have characterized much of Christian history—with impunity, even self-righteousness! "Those who kill you will think that by doing so they are offering worship to God" (John 16:2). How could we so miss the point?

The truth is, the only school in which we learn to know and love God is the school of humanity, our daily and practical road to enlightenment. For Christians this is the way of Incarnation, where we begin and where we end. "We know that we have passed from death to life because we love one another" (1 John 3:14). Love, more than any dogma or church affiliation, is our only proof that we belong to God.

What do I do or say that tears down other people?
How can I change that behavior?

DAY 178

THE ONLY WAY

As we make our way on the spiritual path, it's worth noting that every biblical hero, at some point on the journey, was forced to leave the worlds of position, privilege, perk, and power, to be able to hear and speak the truth at a deeper level. We can pay a high price for spiritual transformation.

Here is where we join Joseph, thrown into the pit by his brothers; Jonah thrown into the belly of the beast by his shipmates; Jeremiah thrown into the muddy cistern by his religious denomination; Job thrown onto the dunghill by his own self-doubt; and Jesus on the cross, carrying the absurdity and evil of the whole lot.

These seem to be the scenarios of those who follow God's way. The price is higher than any of us (except perhaps Jesus) would choose alone. Note that in many cases, circumstances or other people force our suffering.

When have I been forced to leave position, privilege, perk, or power? What happened?

DAY 179

HOW GOD TEACHES

Why would a man, secure and happy with his life, descend calmly and confidently from the tower of his success? It may arrive as darkness, uncertainty, an opening, or great enthusiasm, but now and then a new horizon is offered to a man's soul. It's always an invitation, an opportunity for free choice. Accepting the invitation will feel like falling or losing, and the outcome or direction won't be totally clear, if discernible at all.

This strange path will not lead you away from God, or from what matters. I promise you. The journey itself is the growing edge and the destination. It will lead you to love and to God, even though it will feel risky and probably not "religious" at all. This is *the* path of salvation. You won't have a lot of takers or supporters, and you may have well-intentioned critics, like Job's friends. But finally God and grace can steal away your good order, your proper self-image, and all that wholesome religion to offer you the Real Thing.

When has a new opening for life with God
presented itself to me? What did I do?

Day 180

Wholeheartedness

Much of a man's life is spent going to work, running errands, cleaning house, mowing the lawn, waiting in lines, attending meetings, and tending to the necessary but endless minutia that make up life. We know that we can't live as if we're in the middle of an Indiana Jones adventure. We know that much of life is rather dull and repetitive. That's why it's so important to be fully present to the ordinary things that keep us going: a movie, a concert, dinner with a friend. Anything you do fully gives you joy. Anything done halfheartedly will bore you. People do not tire from overwork nearly as much as from halfheartedness. Wholeheartedness requires that a person be fully present. And people who are present are most ready to experience the Presence.

In the middle of the ordinary, in the midst of the tedium, if we pay attention to the Presence, we will be blessed by joy, grace, and simple, sustaining pleasures. We no longer need religious highs to know God; the lows and mediums are more than high enough.

How can I go about my ordinary life
more wholeheartedly?

Day 181

Failing and Falling

Young men need to know that it's inevitable they will fail, and it's all right that they fail. We need to provide a net so that they can enter defeat with understanding, courage, and wisdom.

Generally, twelve-step groups are doing a better job than religious groups at helping people in this regard. They provide members with a net that allows them to fall into the necessary pit of failure. For addicts, it is often abject failure—hitting bottom, losing everything meaningful—that becomes a person's entrance to real and deeper life. I would hope that everyone does not have to become an addict to face their shadow self, to learn humility, and to discover their Higher Power in an active and trustful way.

But there needs to be something *to gain our attention, to humiliate our false self, and to focus our deepest desire.* Without it, much religion is mere fire insurance. This saying is worth repeating: Religion is populated by people who are afraid of hell. Spirituality begins when we have been through hell.

When have I failed, and what did I gain
from the failure?

Day 182

The Sun Is Dying Too

The sun is dying, ever so slowly. Every second, it transforms four million tons of itself into light, which sustains everything on this planet. In this universe, each form of liquid, gas, or solid lasts for a while but eventually (maybe over millions of years) loses its form and becomes something else. The dying is often violent, seemingly wasteful, and utterly inefficient. We humans have learned to love the forms, and we find it tragic when they change and pass. Yet they always do, and we suffer the pain of loss. We would never suffer if first we did not love.

So everything, not just Jesus, goes through the cycle of passion, death, and resurrection. He came to tell us not to avoid it, that we cannot avoid it—and in fact, faith is the act of trusting the process and finding God in this "paschal mystery" of loss and renewal. It will always be a mystery, which will elicit deep resistance from humans. Jesus had to walk it personally and dramatically himself to show us that it was okay.

When have my attachments brought me pain?

DAY 183

WHAT'S THE QUESTION?

Most people of faith believe that God is the answer, but do we ask ourselves: What is the actual question?

Does God just need us to know that he exists? Is God so insecure that he needs us to get his name right? Is "God" simply the correct answer to the biggest SAT question of all? Does God exist so we can think correctly about him or her? Would the God who created billions of galaxies really be that worried about our little PR campaigns in his favor? Why would the God who created mountains, moonrises, and peacocks need us to tell the world who he is? Does God really need *me* to get it right and to share my understanding with others?

When looking at the history of religion and the history of violence, we see how they have consistently overlapped. We see that correct answers have not always created loving or dedicated people or a healed world. We suspect that too many people with answers have never asked the right questions.

What questions guide my life right now?

DAY 184

MALE RITUAL

Personal breakdown often leads to spiritual breakthrough. But such passages need to be ritualized in some way, or the dramatic message is not perceived, remembered, or allowed to transform us.

Our culture does a poor job of teaching men appropriate rituals; that's the job of spiritual elders and initiators. Yet soul initiation has not been deemed necessary in the West for some centuries now. The church's initiation rites (baptism, communion, and confirmation) became so pretty and clerical that most laymen do not relate to them seriously.

Our church rituals became more about joining the group than changing your life, certainly not joining him in the tomb and dying with him (Romans 6:4) or anything most men remember. Men will not really pay attention unless the rituals are clear and brutally honest. Is it any accident that the one ritual men show up for is being marked for death on Ash Wednesday? And it is not even a holy day of obligation.

What ritual have I participated in lately? What ritual do I feel that I need right now?

Day 185

Gods Who Shit

One wonderful result of initiation is the gut experience that your life is not all about you. You are about Life! Can you make that switch? You are a glorious part of creation, but you're not the center of anything. An effective initiation aligns you correctly inside the universe; you belong more than ever, but you no longer see yourself as the reference point. You are both a beloved son of God and a "little shit," as I love to say. I got the phrase from Ernest Becker's life-changing book, *The Denial of Death.* He said that the truth we must but cannot reconcile is that we humans are "gods who shit."

I hope you're relieved to make this discovery. You no longer have to fix everything, figure out everything, do it all right, or be anything more than fully human. *You take yourself more seriously now as a beloved son of God, and yet you do not take yourself seriously at all.* This seems like a contradiction only before you are initiated. Afterwards it makes total sense.

In what ways have I realized that life is not about me, but that I'm about life? What is my best response to that insight?

Day 186

A New Kind of Infallibility

The psychologist Carl Jung offered a profound and helpful insight into the dynamic of the human shadow. He said that *the greater the light you have, the greater the shadow you will cast.* People with amazing gifts in one area usually have significant blind spots. I find this consistently to be true, surely in myself. We see this pattern in the Gospel stories of Simon Peter. Jesus proclaims him to be the "rock" upon which the community can be built (Matthew 16:18), yet he is consistently shown to be a flawed and weak human being. His first response is usually wrong, and when it is right, then his second response is wrong (Matthew 16:22–23). Rather amazing that the Roman Church never saw that. It is certainly a strange kind of "infallibility," yet it could be a new kind of infallibility. There is some reason Jesus chose this clearly blessed/flawed individual as the representative for the Twelve originals.

What are my gifts—and what are my shadows?

Day 187

The Search for the Imperfect

We need to know that *the search for the perfect is the most common enemy of the good.* God created humans and named them "very good" (Genesis 1:31) in their human ordinariness. He did not name them perfect or infallible. Our religious search for infallibility and perfection has prevented us from loving and accepting and using what Jesus saw and used and accepted.

Peter was a great light, and he cast a significant shadow. He is the only one Jesus ever calls a devil. Light and darkness can and do coexist in all things human and created. As men grow in wisdom, they see this same infallible pattern in themselves, and they accept this same infallible pattern in everything else in the universe. This is a new and truly helpful kind of infallibility, which keeps us from becoming idolaters.

Where in my life does the need for the perfect become the enemy of the good? Who do I know who is very human, yet an effective man?

Day 188

The Shadow

Jesus used the language of darkness and light several times to talk about the human spiritual condition (e.g., Luke 11:33–36). The reason many of us quote C. G. Jung is that he is often saying a similar thing, but with a contemporary vocabulary we understand.

Jung would say that the shadow is not evil; it's simply where we put our qualities and traits that we deem unacceptable. From our earliest days, authorities and peers let us know the subjects that are out-of-bounds. These issues become exiled to the shadow world. So when the shadow shows itself in individuals, people think *evil!* When groups show the shadow, it can appear to be more legitimate except in extreme cases like vast genocide.

The trouble with the shadow is that it makes us blind to the evil or potential for evil in ourselves. We hurt others, particularly those we love, because we are unaware of our own shadow. So every showing of the shadow is a helpful epiphany. Shadow work is good and important stuff. Marriages and relationships are made-to-order for shadow work.

When have I encountered my shadow side?
What was my response?

Day 189

When Earth and Heaven Meet

On the second day, God separated heaven from earth (Genesis 1:6–8). Genesis does not say that the second day was good, because it is not good to separate heaven from earth. A deep religious experience will reveal that there is only one world, one reality, and it is all "supernatural." We may have initially assumed that there is some clear division between the natural and the supernatural, which is where almost all religion begins, but when we encounter God we realize that any seeming division is an unfortunate illusion.

There is only one world, one history, and it is God's—and it is also ours. Once we realize this union, life changes radically. Trees start shining, and we notice God's fingerprints everywhere. There is only one world in which everything belongs. It is not good when light is separated from darkness, or heaven from earth. Remember, true religion (*re-ligio*, re-ligament) binds it all back together again. This is an immediate result of authentic religious experience, and why it brings such lasting joy.

How have I experienced the one world or one reality? In what ways do I still see the world as natural and supernatural?

Day 190

Deal with It, Man!

Surely you know the saying, "Deal with it, man!" This is good advice, because what we don't deal with will affect us anyway. Suppressing what we don't want to deal with is like trying to hold a basketball underwater while going on with life as usual. You might be able to do it for a while, but when life's challenges and opportunities require your focus, up pops the basketball—often at the most inopportune times.

What we suppress—the shadow aspect of life— ambushes us sooner or later. We don't know why we're depressed or angry, why everyone and everything is out to get us. We may find ourselves responding as if threatened, but we can't acknowledge that we're afraid. Fear has gained a big foothold in the lives of men, precisely because men deny fear and won't deal with it. Then when it pops up like that basketball, we don't even know what it is. We just know we are upset and not in good shape. With nothing else to do, we'll probably look for something to drink.

What fears, anger, or other shadow parts of myself do I try to suppress? How have these things popped up in my life?

Day 191

Humor Is the First Casualty

Can you laugh at yourself? One indication of a large and repressed shadow, both in a person and in a culture, is the lack of a healthy sense of humor. If you or the group you belong to can't laugh at yourselves, you are in trouble. Here is a reliable rule of thumb in the spiritual life: men who can't let others poke fun at them or cannot laugh at themselves always have a large shadow that has been denied and suppressed.

People who are overly stern and moralistic usually have a significant, repressed shadow. They walk through life shaking a judgmental finger in disapproval—and they disapprove of just about everything! They're often incapable of easy enjoyment. They might exhibit in secret the behaviors they so vigorously attack in public. They are split, even from themselves.

A person who can laugh and go with life does not demand to be in control, which is why the most controlling people may be very sarcastic but lack an authentic sense of humor.

When was I recently stern and moralistic? What triggered that reaction? What did it touch within me that might indicate my shadow?

Day 192

Shadow Boxing

It takes so much energy and effort to suppress what we find unacceptable in ourselves that we can have very little energy left for anything else. This is why some people exist in a stew of aimless anxiety, nameless dread, free-floating fear, generalized anger, and irritated exhaustion. These are all indications that we've placed a great portion of our unacceptable self in exile. We have no patience, no forgiveness, no mercy, but only harsh judgments. No gospel.

We then project our own sick symptoms onto the screen of our outer world and call it reality. We don't see the world as it is; we see the world through the prism of our anxiety, fear, and other rejected emotions. This is what creates the worlds of conspiracy theories, militia movements, and the hateful rantings of radio and TV personalities. People are largely fighting their own fears and denied shadow selves. If there is no real shadow boxing with the self, the boxing ring of life becomes scary indeed. This is much of our world, brothers.

What shadows am I fighting right now?

DAY 193

GUILTY AS FEARED

Men out of touch with their shadow tend to feel unnecessarily guilty. They've been burdened with the assumption that they had to be perfect boys and men to please Daddy-God. They may not even know the extent of their guilt or shame because they've repressed it. The need to be perfect and in control at all times cripples their ability to deal with the shadow in a healthy way.

How can we face our shadow self without feeling condemned by it or identifying with it? For people with early religious conditioning, the image of God is often the root of the problem. If we think God loves only perfect people, we will try to disown our imperfections. But what kind of small and weak God would that be? Didn't Jesus offer us a more radically compassionate image of God—a God who delights in us? Do we believe Jesus or emotional conditioning? Please hear this, from the saints and mystics: God never leads the soul through guilt, shame, or fear, but attracts the soul through love.

How do you believe God responds to your imperfections, foibles, and sins? How does your sense of God line up with what Jesus taught about the father?

DAY 194

THE LOG IN YOUR OWN EYE

There are a lot of enraged people walking around pretending they're not angry—and everybody can see it except them.

Why is shadow work so important? We need to acknowledge, forgive, and heal all that lurks in our shadow, or we will continue to distort reality by projecting all that we hate from within ourselves onto other people and the world around us. We will objectify and demonize an individual or a group, never understanding that what we hate in another is merely what we hate in ourselves. If you think this is merely modern psychology, read Matthew 7:1–5 about the log and the splinter. Jesus says clearly that evil is first of all in the eye of the beholder.

Therapy, pastoral counseling, men's work, contemplative prayer, spiritual direction, and volunteer work are all ways to forgive and heal within ourselves the hatred, anger, long-suppressed disappointments, and broken dreams we've carried for too long. Then we will no longer need to project our pain onto the world. Then we can be at peace. Really!

What negative qualities am I quick to see in others? How could I work with my shadow rather than fight or suppress it?

Day 195

Face the Shadow

Face the shadow, but do not identify with it. It represents only part of who you are. Identifying with the shadow leads to much evil in the world. People see themselves as only shadow, and they become attached to, and driven by, fear, guilt, and shame.

If we can meet the shadow, our response likely will be, not anger, but sadness. Men can experience days of deep sorrow after encountering what they've hidden from themselves for so long. We get a glimpse of how broken we are.

The hero in us will want to attack, fix, or deny the existence of what is in the shadow. Or he will be tempted to share dramatically everything about it as a way to control it. The saint merely weeps over the shadow and forgives it—and at the same time forgives himself for being human. He opens his arms to that which has been in exile and welcomes it home. For St. Francis this was symbolized by his embrace and kissing of a leper, which he considered the moment of his conversion.

When I encounter the shadow aspects of myself, what is my first response? What are some healthy ways I could respond to the shadow?

Day 196

What Morality Means

Jesus understood the need to make friends with the shadow. Understanding how the shadow operates is a necessary breakthrough if we are to understand the real meaning of morality and of the moral quest. Jesus captured this insight very clearly in several parables, especially in the story of the man who sows good seed in his field (Matthew 13:24–30) but still finds weeds among the wheat.

Most of us are like the man who sowed the seed. We're considered good men and good citizens. We go to church, provide for our families, work hard, and stay out of trouble. Then one disturbing day someone points out to us that there are weeds growing in the midst of our wheat. "Where did the weeds come from?" the servant asks the master. And we are surprised, perhaps disappointed, that anyone else would notice what we thought was not there or what we had hidden so well. "Some enemy must have done this!" is his first response. *Surely not me*, we sincerely think.

What weeds have cropped up in my life?

DAY 197

WHO, ME?

When we find weeds in our life, we've received a glimpse of ourselves as we truly are: neither completely good nor bad, but fully human and flawed. This could begin our grand adventure of exploring the interior life.

Our immediate impulse will be to pull out the weeds. It's shocking to see ourselves clearly for the first time—we're so much like the very people we look down on! What we need is help from someone wise and discerning—what a good confessor, father figure, or mentor is supposed to be. They know how to turn soil into soul, and grit into grace.

In the parable, the worker who discovers the weeds wants to rip them out immediately. But the master tells him, "No," don't even imagine such a thing, "for in gathering the weeds you would uproot the wheat along with them" (Matthew 13:29). He advises the worker to "let both of them grow together until the harvest" when God will sort them out (13:30). Why didn't someone ever tell me that?

How do I follow Jesus' advice and refrain from pulling up the weeds in my life?

Day 198

Which Are the Weeds?

Jesus tells us to wait until the crops have ripened and matured before separating the weeds from the wheat—that is, the bad from the good. We aren't capable of such discernment. We don't know what the real gift is, and we have no clue what our real sin is. What we see as our greatest gift at twenty often turns out to be our greatest fault by midlife. And what first looks like our early sin is later the very thing that collapses us into God! We have to give ourselves time to live into the wisdom of knowing true good and true evil. This is probably why the Bible begins by telling us not to eat of this tree at all (Genesis 2:17)! So the master says to wait and let the reapers sort it out at the harvest (Matthew 13:30).

God is patient and quite willing to work with our honesty and humility, and God includes us in this process of wisdom and growth, through our own recognition, decision, and loving trust.

What about my earlier life do I see differently,
now that I'm a bit older?

DAY 199

LEARNING FROM THE SHADOW

The shadow self is not the evil self; it is the unacceptable self. It's the side of us we don't want to show to the world. But we need to understand that the desirable qualities are invariably accompanied by their opposites, which live in the unconscious or "shadow" self.

The shadow contains all the parts of the self that we have scorned and sent into exile. Yet we must eventually welcome them home because they have essential lessons to teach us. The stones we rejected in the heroic building of our tower in the first half of life become the source of the greatest lessons we need for the next part of the journey. Or as Jesus puts it, "The stone that the builders rejected has become the cornerstone" (Mark 12:10).

In the second half of life, we discover that we have actually been linked to our shadow by our harsh judgments against it, like people who participate in crusades against pornography or homosexuality, while being secretly involved themselves. (Read Ephesians 5:11–14 for a good scriptural meditation on this.)

What aspects of myself did I reject early on but which have turned out to be useful in later experience?

Day 200

If You Spot It, You Got It

If we don't confront the shadow in ourselves, we'll spend our time and energy despising or fearing the same material in others. We can't help but be fascinated when we see evidence of our game playing in other people, and our first instinct is to attack or expose it. If you find yourself railing against someone else, or lost in conspiracy theories and paranoia, odds are that you're seeing your own issues in that situation. Once you see it clearly, the game is over. Shadowy material needs to stay in the dark to survive, which is why the Scriptures are always telling you to come into the light, why Jesus tells demons to "show themselves," and why the twelve-step program says that "you are as sick as your secrets."

Given the faults I notice in others, what might be existing in my shadow self?

DAY 201

LEARNING TO LAUGH

Facing your shadow is the task of a lifetime, and it demands courage, humility, patience, and compassion for yourself. It will never stop but will take you deeper and deeper as you learn to patiently grieve over your sins, to weep over your silliness, and to confront your inconsistencies and contradictions. It is Paul's thorn in the flesh that keeps him from getting too proud (2 Corinthians 12:7).

In the end, you will actually learn to laugh at your shadow games. Laughing at the shadow self is the final freedom and victory over it: you see it, name it, recognize the illusions, and then laugh at your poverty and weakness. *Laughing happens only when you no longer need to hate or attack things, but you have clearly spotted the game and are thus free from it.* Maybe this is exactly what Jesus meant when he said "Weep now, for you will laugh" (Luke 6:21).

Which games and illusions in my shadow self can I name? Am I ready to laugh at them yet?

Day 202

Shadow and Persona

In the first half of life, the young man dutifully builds his tower, but he is simultaneously constructing his shadow self and doesn't realize it. You see, *shadow and persona are correlative terms*. Persona is the chosen self-image that you want to project, and the way that you want others to think about you. The stronger you are attached to any persona ("mask" in Greek), the more shadow self you will have. The less persona you are attached to, usually the less shadow self. Much of Jesus' advice about not doing good things in public "for others to see" is precisely addressing this issue. Thus saints such as St. Francis and St. Philip Neri would go out of their way to walk through town advertising that they were *not* saintly or holy! (Walking in underwear and playing childish games being Francis's cover, while dirty jokes and wine bottles were Philip Neri's disguise!)

---

*How would I describe my persona—the self
I want to show the world?*

Day 203

Laughing and Weeping

A man desperately seeking to maintain and project a certain image of himself can never laugh at himself. Equally tragic is that he can't weep over his mistakes or anyone else's; he must fix or change them. He is too needy of being perfect, too earnest, too "moral," and too full of himself—thus, the pain of the world can't reach him nor can he be sympathetic to others.

A man so dependent on his own image is likely to pursue salvation compulsively. He must "be saved," has to do whatever is required for holiness, for success, for being right. He can neither weep nor laugh, because he cannot imagine being loved except by trying real hard. Grace has become an impossibility, and it is grace that engenders both laughter and tears.

Am I pursuing salvation? How am I trying to be who I want to be?

Day 204

Cultures Have Shadows, Too

Shadows are carried not only by individuals but by cultures as well. Societies have their secrets and denials. Every group, nation, religion, and race has taboo subjects that they corporately agree not to talk about. In Victorian England, for example, body fluids or body functions were never to be spoken of in public. All was externally proper and polite. Miss Manners was in charge of everything. However, England exported its shadow issues out to its colonies, where "improper" peoples could be subjected, enslaved, and sexually abused.

All groups, organizations, and cultures have a social face. Everything that seems unsuitable goes underground. Our uncivilized desires and feelings, the identities we don't want, are hidden in the shadow world. Soon we forget the shadow's existence, and we believe our public image. When that happens, a group or nation is capable of doing great evil without recognizing it as evil.

God sends prophets to make nations aware of their shadow side, which usually results in the prophets getting persecuted or killed.

What are some of the elements that your culture keeps in shadow? What helps you recognize these elements?

Day 205

Neither Offensive nor Defensive

When we become aware of our shadow, the temptation is to fight it. But know this: *the shadow always turns to us the same face we turn to it.* If we are gentle with our shadow, it will be gentle with us. If we learn to embrace it and forgive it, miraculously, it will forgive us. If we can find compassion for what we discover about ourselves, our shadow will respond with compassion.

But if out of fear we attack our shadow, our shadow will attack us back. It will ambush us when we least expect it. Although we're polishing the false front we've created for our life, our shadow will sneak up on us from behind. *Whenever you find yourself especially defensive, you have usually just been confronted with your shadow.*

The spiritual life is a great recycler; nothing really goes away. Everything that has happened to us remains, and if not healed, will just keep showing itself in newly disguised forms. Robert Bly says that you don't ever fully get rid of your demons, you just educate them.

Which face—anger or compassion—am I offering
my shadow right now?

DAY 206

LIGHTEN UP!

Although portraits of saints usually depict them as sad-faced and dour, their biographies reveal them to be full of light and laughter. What did they know that we don't know?

People who channel a lot of energy into repressing their shadow tend to be serious and heavy. It takes so much energy to keep the heavy lid on our dark side that we have very little energy left for anything happy, beautiful, or fun. People repressing a huge shadow usually lack enthusiasm and a relaxed sense of humor. Their days are a series of life-and-death moral issues, everything is a cause, and they rarely lighten up. Everything is monumental, when it does not need or deserve to be.

Did you ever see a picture of the Dalai Lama? He's always smiling. One cannot but feel that he has faced his shadow and forgiven it. It releases all kinds of life energy for compassion and joy.

Who brightens my life with laughter and enjoyment? Am I able to live that way, too, and if not, why not?

Day 207

Fear Not

Fear has gotten a free ride in our culture because we never recognized it as one of the capital sins. The Enneagram system of discernment tells us that probably 50 percent of people are fear-based. With that much fear around, it has to be disguised as "prudence," "good stewardship," or "common sense." Politicians, pundits, advertisers, and media moguls all seem invested in ratcheting up people's sense of panic, because they know how well it works.

Unacknowledged fear stifles relationships, openness, and love. It's hard to grow in charity and justice if you're afraid of everything and everybody. You are closed down and defensive and unable to trust the moment. Anxiety is probably a more accurate word for this kind of constant, aimless fear and self-doubt. Such unrecognized turmoil will control us. Thus the New Testament warns us more than eighty times to avoid fear. Jesus is constantly encouraging his followers: "Fear not," "Be not afraid," "Do not let your hearts be troubled." Yet I have never heard of any Christian accused of the "sin" of fear.

What am I afraid of? How deep is this fear, and how long have I struggled with it?

DAY 208

GUILT VERSUS SHAME

Let's distinguish between good guilt, bad guilt, and shame. Good guilt is the necessary sense of conscience that tells me to take responsibility for my mistakes. Good guilt is an appropriate response to something I've done or thought that was wrong. Shame, however, causes me to feel bad *about who I am as a person*, apart from anything I've done or thought. If I carry shame, I'll see almost everything as something to feel guilty about. Thus, shame leads to bad, neurotic guilt, which doesn't bring me to truth or to God but keeps me feeling defeated and inferior.

After forty years of ministry I say confidently: *God never leads the soul by guilt or shame*. Even appropriate guilt, which helps me, does not lead to deeper love of God.

God leads the soul through seduction, invitation, self-exposure, unearned grace, deep forgiveness, and growing acceptance of me in my brokenness—which is what entices me away from mistakes almost without my realizing it. I would love to convince people of this almost more than anything else!

How can guilt become a form of self-importance?
How do I use guilt to avoid my own growth?

Day 209

Anger and Sadness

Some men go through life in a state of free-floating, generalized anger. They easily find people, situations, and inanimate objects to which they attach their anger. Usually there is much unresolved and hidden hurt in their past—rejection, failure, guilt, shame, oppression, abuse, or betrayal. As always, it does not go away; it just festers until it is brought into the light and healed.

I want you to notice the more subtle feelings behind your anger, because anger often serves as an all-purpose default setting in many a man's emotional life. In fact, many angry men are actually deeply sad, but they don't know it. They don't know how to feel sadness, which is considered weakness, so they default to anger, and never get to the real issue that is making them so unhappy. At times I've thought that probably a third of the men I've met are in this category.

When have I been mad today or this week? What other emotion may the anger have been masking?

Day 210

Make Friends with the Dark Knight

The less aware we are of our shadow self, the more damage it will do. Church teachings on repentance, confession, and forgiveness make good sense. At some point we must say to at least one person: "My name is Joe, and I'm an alcoholic" (or a sex addict, or a workaholic, or an unloving man). Bring it out of darkness, and "everything that becomes visible is light" (Ephesians 5:14).

That's what we mean by making friends with the shadow. The hero in the Holy Grail stories was advised not to kill the Dark Knight but to make friends with him. It took me years to comprehend this, but now I wonder if there is any other way to overcome evil except to make it work for you and get it on your side. That's what Jesus did on the cross by making his own murder the salvation of the world. He didn't destroy his killers, but forgave them because "they do not know what they are doing" (Luke 23:34). The shadow never knows what it is doing.

In what ways have I confessed my sins and brought my darkness into the light?

Day 211

Is Change a Way of Life?

I always wondered why Jesus' opening line was "repent" (Matthew 4:17 and Mark 1:15). The word *metanoia* is a Greek word that means "to turn around," although it literally means to "go beyond the mind." The call to an utterly new mind, to turn around and begin again, is at the beginning of the Gospel and is the essence of a man's journey to find his true self. He needs a whole new receiver to even pick up the new message, and then this receiver seems to need constant updates, or it returns to its one preferred frequency.

But how many times do we have to turn around and start again? How many updates do we need? How many times must we change? Isn't it just one decision for Jesus or one joining of the church? No, it seems that the whole journey is about letting go and developing an ongoing willingness to turn around one more time. We keep hoping to see and think and live with God's heart. As the Shakers used to sing, "The turning never stops."

When was the last time I experienced any kind of new mind or turning? What kind of turning do I need to do now?

Day 212

DREAMS

How can you learn more about your hidden self? One powerful way our shadow reveals itself is through our dreams. Dreams play an important role throughout the Bible. Even today, sometimes dreams are the only way God can break through to us.

Some dreams are disturbing because they represent shadow energy. But simply observe the characters and events. Become a detective. Reflect on the dream as well as your emotional reaction to it and ask, "What is this trying to tell me?" Think of your dreams as valuable lessons, gifts from God that arrive during the night when the boundary between consciousness and the unconscious is more permeable. That is why truth can break in through dreams.

One thing I've come to notice in my dreams is that they are hardly ever judgmental or moralistic. *They simply reveal.* It is my work to make connections and decisions. In fact, this has been so consistent in my dream life that I see it as evidence that God does not judge or moralize. God reveals, and leaves the invitation open-ended.

What do my dreams reveal about my shadow self?

DAY 213

NEITHER ATTACHING NOR DETACHING

There are two counterproductive ways to deal with the shadow and with all emotions. One is to repress things too quickly, the strategy of the conservative personality. The other is to express things too quickly, the strategy of the liberal personality. Neither strategy works well because neither teaches us what we can learn from the situation.

The challenge is to hold things in the middle—don't vent and get too invested in your feelings ("acting out"), and don't push them down and think they will go away ("denial"); just stay with them and let them *settle and become clear.* When we hold such a creative tension and refrain from either too much expression or too much repression, true learning and deeper spirituality can unfold. Otherwise, we merely prolong the problem.

This is hard work, a real challenge. But having the discipline, patience, and faith to neither hold on nor push down can be the beginning of what we mean by "the discernment of spirits," which is one of the gifts of the Holy Spirit (1 Corinthians 12:10).

When am I most likely to repress? When am I most likely to express? What would happen if I refrained from both responses?

Day 214

The Task within the Task

Many of us were trained to "get rid of our sins." There was little or no education in seeing our sins as symptoms and learning what the symptoms had to tell us. Many of us never learned the difference between what we said, even to ourselves, and what was really going on. We learned laws but not spiritual discernment.

Two people can be performing the exact same job description according to the law, but by looking closely you can see that one employee builds trust, confidence, and teamwork while the other stirs discontent, gossip, and unhappiness. *These are the tasks within the tasks, and in fact, they are what you're really getting for your money.* Only a discerning person will see this and address it appropriately. We will be less concerned with getting rid of the sins and more interested in dealing with the knowledge these symptoms provide.

When have I reacted to sin without understanding what that symptom was telling me?

DAY 215

PLASTIC MEN

Some men push their shadow down so far that it's all but annihilated. They've turned into smiling, sweet, plastic men, sometimes very religious. There's nothing real or rugged about them. They are too good to be true. For example, there's the man who cannot get angry with his wife or anybody. She carries all the anger in the relationship and becomes the archetypal witch. He denies his own anger—even as it grows and grows—because he piously believes anger is always wrong and is beneath him. His anger is his shadow self. He looks good, she looks bad, but what is the truth? To him, Jesus might well say, "Consider whether the light in you is not darkness" (Luke 11:35).

Wrestling with the shadow is the dominant spiritual task of life. It's what gives us a tangible self, one that is anything but plastic. Wrestling with your shadow gives you flesh and blood. And people will more likely take you seriously, warts and all.

How have I truly wrestled with life? What tempts me to avoid the wrestling?

DAY 216

THE PREREQUISITE

How do we begin facing our own dark side? First things first: We cannot face the dark at any depth until we have seen some real light. We will not have the courage to face the shadow until we've experienced some unconditional love in our life, from God or friends. Until then, we don't have the guts to do the hard work of the soul. This helps us be patient with people living at a survival level who have no courage or encouragement to do their shadow work.

We must discover a source of inner security before we can withstand the insecurities that every life holds. Children are not ready for this, nor are teenagers, nor are young adults. Honest soul work is usually done in the second half of life, although it is forced on some much earlier through imprisonment or family tragedy.

Have I tried to face the shadow before I've grown confident in God's love for me? How can I develop more awareness of this great and unconditional love?

Day 217

Both Are True

God's love allows you to embrace all that you are: both the light and the dark. A mature spirituality calls you to own both sides of your life—at once.

And you know what? If there is one thing harder than owning your dark side, it is believing with all your heart that you are much more a Son of the Light (1 Thessalonians 5:5) and rejoicing that your name is already "written in heaven" (Luke 10:20).

Do I believe that I am a Son of the Light?
What, really, do I believe?

Day 218

Transformation

All human transformation takes place inside liminal space. The Latin word *limen* means "threshold." Liminality is an inner state and sometimes an outer situation in which people can begin to think and act in genuinely new ways. It is the state of being betwixt and between, of having left one room but not having entered the next room yet. You are poised at a new starting gate, although you usually do not know it. In fact, you are normally upset and out of balance for a while.

Liminal space occurs only when our comfort zone has collapsed. This includes any hiatus between stages in life: separation or divorce, job change, illness, loss, death, failure of any kind. It is a graced time during which we are not certain of our next move, when we're not in control, when something genuinely new can happen. If God wants to get to you, which God always does, the chances are best during any liminal time. Otherwise, you remain on continuous cruise control.

What has been my experience of living
in liminal space?

Day 219

Displacement as Liminal Space

Much of the work attributed to God in the Bible is designed to lead people into liminal space, to keep them there long enough to learn something new, and eventually to lead them back out. Dramatic symbols might be the Israelites in Egypt, Daniel in the lion's den, Susanna falsely accused, Elijah in the cave, Peter and Paul in prison. Liminal space is the great teachable space, the ultimate threshold of transformation.

Many spiritual giants have tried to live their lives in permanent liminality. They try to live on the margins and on the periphery of the system so they will not get sucked into its illusions and payoffs. They deliberately live "off balance" from what most of us take for normal and common sense. Think of the radical poverty of St. Francis, the inner city hospitality of Dorothy Day, the lives of almost all missionaries. They know that some kind of displacement from business as usual is the only way to ensure deeper wisdom and broader compassion.

Whom do I know who spends a lot of time in transformational space?

Day 220

Make Time to Waste Time

For those of us who cannot easily head off to the wilderness or the cloister for long stretches of time, traditional religions offered opportunities for temporary and partial liminality. They encouraged occasional or seasonal practices such as pilgrimages, silent retreats, and periods of ritual fasting such as Lent and Ramadan. Unfortunately, once-a-week church services do not come close to creating liminal space. In fact, people tend to get upset if you change their expected order of service! That is how small our comfort zones often are.

There has to be something different and daring—even nonsensical—to awaken us from our comfortable sleepwalk. Liminal space always feels counterintuitive, like a waste of time. It doesn't correspond to the logic of our normal way of proceeding. And that's the point. Entering liminal space breaks our sense of practicality and function, and it moves us into what seems like a shapeless world where totally new questions—and answers—tend to arise. In any "shapeless" world we will have to "change shapes" to survive or enjoy. That is what we mean by transformation.

What liminal spaces or times have
I created or discovered?

Day 221

Standing in the Threshold

In liminal space, we face the things we can't do anything about (fateful things) and the things we can't do anything with (useless things). It is the *fateful or useless things that invariably do something with us*. God, says St. John of the Cross, is by definition the "unfamiliar," always beyond the expected and ordinary. So we must go there.

We need to break out of our accustomed patterns, become uncomfortable, in order to be granted new eyes. We need to fast instead of eat; maintain silence instead of talk; experience emptiness instead of fullness, anonymity instead of persona, poverty instead of plenty. In any chosen liminal space, we descend and intentionally do not immediately come back up or out; we seek status reversal instead of status, and social displacement instead of social belonging. We used to call such things "urban plunges" when we went to live in the inner city. It is first of all scary but invariably quite rewarding by the end. You really do change.

Then you can reenter the old world with new freedom and spontaneity.

---

*Where can I find liminal space? Can I create it,
or should I simply look for it right where I am?*

Day 222

Retreats Can Be Advances

When we choose to go to liminal space, we are choosing the chaos of the unconscious over explanations and easy answers. We are breaking our addiction to see if we can find God in what seems like disorder. We soon need new vocabulary and new images to describe our state—the language of darkness rather than light, of wasteland rather than garden, emptiness rather than fullness, deep silence rather than words. Or in the reverse, it might also be garden instead of wasteland or light instead of darkness! Instead of "retreats" they often become advances. What starts as an "outward bound" experience can often lead us inward.

Men have to be encouraged and guided in how to function in such an uneasy place. In many male initiations, boys were left to sit in meaningless silence for days—until they actually yearned for direction and guidance and purpose. We will almost always need encouragement and group cooperation in creating and maintaining what seem like artificial boundaries of silence, solitude, fasting, or "doing nothing." Very few do it effectively alone.

Am I yet yearning for guidance, or do I still feel comfortable with answers and words?

Day 223

Accept No Cheap Substitutes

The most common substitute for liminal space is known as *liminoid* space. Events and occasions that occur in liminoid space look liminal but aren't. Nothing new can happen in liminoid space, only more of the same. We as a culture have become expert at passing off counterfeit experiences for the real thing. Entertainment serves as worship, loud music and big crowds substitute for depth or breadth, and spectacles substitute for any true catharsis.

Fr. Jim Clarke, an elder for the organization Rites of Passage, taught us the difference between ceremony and ritual. Ceremony is meant to maintain the status quo, but *ritual always reveals the shadow and is meant to change us or at least transition us.*

True ritual, like true drama, always creates a catharsis, or emotional cleansing. We prefer ceremony to ritual because it asks so little of us; we merely have to show up physically and be entertained. True ritual demands psychic and personal participation, maybe even a change of heart or mind, whereas the liminoid character of ceremony allows us to observe at a distance.

What experiences in my life would I describe as liminoid?

PART 4

The Paradox of Transformation—Change, Suffering, and Freedom

Final authority about the spiritual journey comes not from any kind of success but from suffering and failure— and what you do with it.

—Richard Rohr

+ The reason there is sin and suffering in the world is not because we are weak, but rather because we are human.

+ Learn the stories of others, listen to them, accept them, understand them—this is the most transformative thing you can do for another.

+ Transformation happens in the presence of images—look around you to see the face of the God you believe in.

+ Spirituality is a process of two steps forward and three back. The three back are the most important.

+ All great spirituality is about learning to let go.

+ Evil is part of life, but evil is not decisive.

+ Transformation includes acknowledging the reality of evil and trusting that God can use even evil to bring about good.

+ There is no freedom or salvation until we've failed.

Day 224

The Sacramental Imagination

Religion is really about one thing: awakening our souls so they will be ready when the Teacher arrives. Religion (*religio*) means to religament or rebind what has been separated. Religion's job description is always the same: To make one out of two. To reconnect what has been disconnected. To heal what has been divided.

Mature religion does this through the magic of word and story and image. Catholics call this "sacrament." Sacramental imagination teaches us how to see, how to see everything, and how to see everything all the way through. It overcomes the divide between sacred and secular, between matter and Spirit, between human and divine.

Once you develop a sacramental imagination, it's difficult to ever go back into a split world. The physical world becomes the best doorway to the divine, and there are no longer just seven ecclesial sacraments, but now seven thousand life sacraments.

Where does sacramental imagination
happen for me?

DAY 225

RETURNING THE DIVINE GAZE

In Ephesians 5:14, St. Paul makes the remarkable statement that "everything that becomes visible is light." In the purest form, prayer is merely the returning of the divine gaze, and we become its reflection, almost in spite of ourselves. Paul states this directly in 2 Corinthians 3:18: "And all of us, with unveiled faces, seeing the glory of the Lord as though reflected in a mirror, are being transformed into the same image from one degree of glory to another."

It's important that we don't trivialize the word *prayer* by turning it into simply a means to get what we want, or to make announcements to God, who already knows (Matthew 6:8). We should consider *prayer* the umbrella word for all the interior journeys or practices that allow us to experience faith, hope, and love. When we think in these terms, we can see that the male spiritual journey should and can be one big prayer. In time, it is no longer something you do, but something you are all the time, as your very life returns the gaze.

How have I brought my journey into the light?
How have I experienced prayer?

Day 226

The Paradox of Grace

According to a certain theology, when a man sins he is punished, and when he is good, he is rewarded. This makes sense. But it isn't what the sages, saints, or Scriptures tell us about God. This "theology" is designed to urge us to save ourselves, and unfortunately this is the theology that many men live by: we get back as good as we give to God. This means that our salvation depends totally on us and on our ability to become perfect, or at least good, men. Thank God, it's not true.

This is not what Jesus teaches us. It's much truer to say that our weakness and brokenness bring us to God—exactly the opposite of what most of us believe. It can take a lifetime, even with grace, to accept such a paradox. *Grace creates the very emptiness that grace alone can fill.*

St. Paul stated this with elegant concision: "'For power is made perfect in weakness.' . . . For whenever I am weak, then I am strong" (2 Corinthians 12:9–10).

When has my brokenness brought God closer? Am
I still trying to earn my own salvation, or am
I relying on God's ability to make me strong
in my weakness?

Day 227

The Economy of Grace

Love can happen only in realms of freedom. Without inner freedom on both sides there can be no true love relationship—only duty, fear, or obligation. So *it is all a matter of growing in freedom*, which could be called "growing in grace."

God's love is perfectly free. It is not coerced by any of our good actions, nor can we lose it because of our bad actions. We are stuck with it and cannot increase—or decrease—God's love for us by anything we do or don't do.

This is God's "eternal covenant" with the soul. God does not love us because God has to; God loves us because God wants to. This frees us to simply receive that love, rather than feverishly try to make ourselves worthy of it.

When am I most able to believe not in my own goodness but in God's?

Day 228

Mystics and Saints

We must not lose hope: God is always and forever at work in the soul and in history. Even this secular world continues to produce mystics and saints.

Men and women are still falling in love with God, especially after they realize how much God has loved them when they were unlovable—and how God trusted them when they could not trust themselves, and how God forgave them when they could not forgive themselves. Be honest, what else would make you fall in love with God?

Have I encountered any mystics and saints on my journey? If so, how have they changed me?

Day 229

Teaching and Sharing

People who insist on teaching us instead of sharing with us can arouse our curiosity, make us think, stir up our minds and souls—and this is no small accomplishment. But often, what they have to say never takes deep root in us. That's a risk I take in writing these meditations.

The people most likely to change our hearts are those who share with us, who walk with us, and who love us. These are the people we can imagine changing our lives for.

Pope Paul VI said it well: "The world will believe teachers only if they have first been witnesses." So I hope you meet some living examples of my many words here, or they will just remain words.

Do I share or do I teach what I most want to pass on to my brothers?

DAY 230

THE PROBLEM OF EVIL

How do good men deal with the problem of evil? We look at an event and its aftermath, such as the earthquake in Haiti, the tsunami in the Pacific, Hurricane Katrina, or horrific events on the local evening news, and eventually we have to ask ourselves, "Where is God in all of this?"

Here is the way I see it play out in real life. People receive the grace to bear whatever comes their way, but the grace may not come until the moment they need it, and it demands collapsing into a Larger Self. That is God's answer. *It is never theoretical but entirely practical and specific!* In other words, the problem of evil cannot be dealt with on the theoretical or universal level, where there is never a satisfying answer. Evil is addressed one person and one day at a time, exactly as Jesus did in his lifetime.

When I confront evil on a tragic scale or on a personal scale, what is my reaction? What am I prepared to do to help? How often do I actually encounter evil in my day-to-day existence?

Day 231

Christian Evolution

Scripture tells us that God created the world and "it was good" and even "very good" (Genesis 1). But that's not always our experience. Is it possible that our definition of good is too narrow? Good equals *harmony and order now*— doesn't it?

Could it be that the good referred to in Scripture is that all things are *capable* of being transformed into harmony and order? The seed of goodness is planted from the beginning, but we are included in the calling forth of this potential.

What if our task is to help God bring about the good? Paul says just that in Romans 8:28: By turning everything to your good, God *cooperates with* all those who love him. I believe this is the deepest Christian meaning of evolution. Creation is not done in one "big bang," but God creates creatures who then join God and cooperate in creating further! Doesn't that make perfect sense? Isn't that wonderful? Isn't that what you do with your own children—on your good days? Well, every day is a good day for God.

How have I brought about order and harmony in the situations around me? What might I do here and now to make things good?

Day 232

Getting the Devil to Work for Good

One of the Bible's most sophisticated and subtle illustrations of evil is found in the parable of the man who sows good seed in his field (Matthew 13:24). In the night, his enemies sow weeds among the wheat. When the owner's servants discover this, they want to pull up the weeds. But the owner says no, "you'll pull up the wheat along with the weeds." He tells them to wait until harvest, and then they can separate the wheat from the weeds. The story encourages us not to take our judgments too seriously or to act on them too quickly.

The key moral question for our time is not how we get rid of evil but rather how we can use it for good. How can we get the devil to work for us, as it were? That is precisely the function of forgiving offenses, forgiving faults, forgiving ourselves, and forgiving enemies. *When you forgive anything, you co-opt the bad event for divine purposes!* That's one reason I cannot give up on Jesus or the Gospels.

In what situation am I having to let the weeds grow along with the wheat?

Day 233

Let Jesus Weep

Our desire for an orderly life and universe can sometimes sacrifice truth and compassion.

When Jesus was looking down on Jerusalem and weeping over it (Luke 19:41), the last thing he needed was a pious man running up to him and saying, "Now, Lord, don't cry. It's all part of God's perfect plan." No, let Jesus weep. The bigger problem is that we do not join with him in weeping over history, humanity, and what we have done to one another and the universal "city" that he stares at. In fact, his very next words are, "If you had only recognized on this day the things that make for peace!" (19:42).

Weeping is a different way of understanding reality. We don't try to fix, explain, or exert control. We probably need to cry much more, not less.

Am I comfortable enough to allow myself the gift of tears when weeping is what's needed? When I don't allow myself to weep, what happens inside me?

Day 234

Living without Answers

Are you willing to say, "I know God is somehow, some-where in this situation. I trust that it will work out; I just don't understand how, but I'm willing to wait"? This attitude is important and the reason we use "journey" language so much in men's work. "The faith and the love and the hope are all in the waiting. Wait without thought, for you are not ready for thought," says T. S. Eliot in *Four Quartets*.

A man who is willing to wait without answers opens a bigger space in which God can create great faith within him. Faith is not the result of any mental process whereby you come to an answer that settles all the dust. If anything, it stirs up the dust in whole new ways.

To build on Eliot, I would say that to believe too quickly is to believe in a small thing, and to believe too easily is to believe in the wrong thing. Faith is a paradox of ground and abyss. It opens deeper questions, but they are questions wor-thy of your soul.

Can I live in the space of not knowing, or do I still push for answers? Am I willing to wait for God, or do I find myself trying to push God as well?

Day 235

Redemptive Listening

We need to learn how to listen to one another without judging or formulating our response. Probably we should allow longer pauses and avoid the immediate and clever comebacks modeled by TV sitcoms. Ultimately, we cannot provide answers for others. But we can walk with them and help them listen to themselves and discover their own answers.

You can tell that many people have not been heard; their compulsive need to be taken seriously often makes them talk too much, too loudly, and too quickly. I confess this is often hard for me, but then I realize that I am far too used to being heard—I speak for a living, plus my parents took me seriously and let me talk.

In the end, what people long for is to be heard, understood, and accepted. It seems that, once someone has truly heard us, we can then begin to hear others, and maybe even ourselves. The most redemptive thing we can do for another person is perhaps just listen and try to understand what he or she needs to say.

When have I experienced another person listening to me at a deep level? When have I truly heard what another person was saying?

Day 236

True Friendship

When we're young, we hope to fall in love with a person who will understand us. When we are understood and feel that another person truly cares for us, it's surprising how many pressing issues seem to lose their weight. Those questions that were haunting us? We don't need the answers anymore. The mere fact that someone else is willing to carry the burden with us and walk with us relieves much of what was troubling us. Presence and companionship are themselves answers!

This is what we need from other men, from the women in our lives, and from friends and family. Humanity asks each of us for simple, caring presence. I can't help but think that many angry people are just very lonely and unaccompanied by anybody's quiet love and strength. This is true friendship. In fact, it's the very shape of divine friendship. God is willing to be with us, which is the promise in almost every biblical theophany: "I will be with you."

When has someone been there for me? When have I accompanied someone else?

DAY 237

THE TWO PATHS

All great spirituality is somehow about letting go. There are two paths that really transform us and make it possible for us to let go: the path of great love and the path of great suffering. Love that does not let go is not really love. And suffering moves us to turn loose out of sheer desperation.

There's no way to plan or program great love or great suffering; each comes on its own terms. There is no precise technique or foolproof formula for great love or great suffering. They are their own teachers, and they instruct us in their own time and in their own way. All we can do is try to be ready to fall, because both love and suffering feel like falling.

How have I experienced letting go? What did it take for me to do that?

Day 238

Grief Work

The typical man comes to consciousness only through grief and concrete forms of suffering, but especially grief he cannot reason his way out of. Grief is the one whack on the side of the head that is strong enough to get men's full attention. It seems to be the price of self-awareness, and it's the crossover point for many from boyhood to manhood. It is a natural initiation.

The young man starts his Icarian flight upward, and perhaps he has to; but until he crashes into the sea, he is largely unconscious and self-absorbed. *Often he has not yet loved anything enough to grieve over its loss.* So he is just a flying boy, and in this age of easy air travel, it is often literally true. The man of some means can just keep traveling to avoid either love, commitment, or the grief that could have come from them—and opened up his soul.

What is my level of self-awareness?

Day 239

The Family Wound

In *Anna Karenina*, Tolstoy wrote, "All happy families are alike; each unhappy family is unhappy in its own way." Now we speak of dysfunctional families. We're wounded by our beginnings, even if we just had a "good-enough father" when we wanted a perfect father. But could it be a necessary wounding?

We are all *living the unlived lives* of our parents and our culture. We're carrying around our own brand of brokenness that makes us yearn and hurt and desire. But when we ache for our mother and father, we express a form of honor toward them. To ache for our own wholeness and to weep over our own lives is probably the necessary fuel that drives us forward. Even to God.

What is my family's wound? Who's unlived life
am I living?

Day 240

Original Sin

Christianity has called our basic wound "original sin." This was an unfortunate choice of words because it implied culpability. We concentrated on an original sin but failed to notice the original blessing (Genesis 1:26–27). But we were trying to make people realistic about their tragic flaw, so that they would not be too surprised or too shocked when it showed itself.

The wound is the unique way through—the only way through—if we are to believe historic male initiation rites. Without exception, the boy was wounded, either ritually, symbolically, or most often physically. Everything pivoted around that. Is it any coincidence that the Christian religion worships a gruesomely wounded man?

If I view sin as woundedness, how will that change the way I deal with it?

Day 241

Faces of the Excluded Ones

What deep gospel truths are we afraid to face as modern men? Did you ever notice that Jesus did not ask or answer the law-and-order questions that culture desires from religion? Jesus never spoke of what we call "family values" or institutional loyalty or national security or war economies, which are now taken for granted as religious values by both churches and politicians. In fact, Jesus was not even a good example of family values: single, celibate, no children, no steady income, and "no place to lay his head."

It's clear that Jesus has a completely opposite agenda, one rejected by the world and much of the church. He asks us to join in solidarity with human weakness and suffering, with the outsiders, the oppressed, and the disadvantaged. If we fail to receive these "sacraments of brokenness" that are all around us, how will we have the courage to discover that we, too, are broken? How will we ever know the suffering face of God, who created them?

In whose face have I seen God this week?

Day 242

The General Dance

If a man has just one moment of authentic spiritual encounter, he knows that he isn't creating it, that it has come from somewhere beyond him, where he is not in control and does not need to be. It is *the* amazing grace. A man then knows he is being led and guided in some great "triumphal procession," as Paul puts it (2 Corinthians 2:14), and he needs only to allow it and participate.

He now understands that he's been invited to what Thomas Merton brilliantly called "The General Dance," where he can now "throw . . . awful solemnity to the winds." His ego naturally shrivels in the experience of such a gratuitous universe, and it's almost a relief to know that he's but a grain of sand in a vast and lovely universe. Now there is no private salvation to achieve or perfect morality to attain. He is happy to join hands in what is happening all the time, everywhere, even without him, but now also with him.

How and when have I experienced the "general dance" of life?

Day 243

Part of the Whole

Mature male spirituality offers men a living connection with the Center and their own center at the same time. It tells us that we are a part of the Whole, yet not the whole. We are not ourselves the Center but we are connected to the Center. We are rightly aligned inside of this one universe! St. Bonaventure said that God is the One "whose center is everywhere and whose circumference is nowhere." When you are connected in this way, indeed everything belongs, and you do too. You do not need to jockey for position, control, or superiority.

The fact that things such as classism, racism, homophobia, war, and consumerism have persisted at such high levels of religion, two thousand years after the incarnation of Jesus, tells me that we are still in the early, maybe even infantile, ages of Christian experience. We do not know that we are already home free, and precisely in our togetherness. How could we have the "perfect happiness of heaven" if we really thought anybody we loved was not there too?

When and how have I experienced a living connection with the Center?

Day 244

Two Economies

When you think you have arrived, soon you will have to face your smallness. You will have to admit that you have miscalculated something important. You've taken yourself much too seriously, or you were simply wrong. This back-and-forth of grace and sin is the living dynamic of the spiritual journey. In the fourth century, St. Gregory of Nyssa said that "sin is a refusal to keep growing up."

This necessary falling becomes the trapdoor through *which you can finally get out of yourself—and through which God can get further in.* The economy of merit is static, small, and self-serving, searching for temporary gains. But grace is a dynamic movement, led by God and disconnected from apparent success. To move from one to the other is the first necessary conversion, then grace will lead you from there. I promise you that.

What kind of conversion have I experienced during the past five years? What happened?

Day 245

The Notion of Sin

Many of us have come to hate the word *sin*; it has been used to blame, exclude, damn, shame, judge by external criteria, and to create separation and superiority.

Jesus faced this problem, too; recall the man born blind (John 9). The disciples wanted to know whose sin had caused the condition—the man's or his parents'. In that culture, people thought sin could be inherited or that it happened within a certain caste or group. This misunderstanding has justified prejudice and hatred throughout history. My hometown sends a group of protesters around the country who carry big signs that read, God Hates Fags.

We must redeem the word and notion of sin, not to condemn or exclude, but to enlighten. Otherwise we will remain dangerously naïve about our potential for evil. If "sin" did not so directly denote "God is upset with you because," we could probably more easily retrain our use of the word. As long as it allows us to speak in the name of God to punish or shame other people, it will be dangerous.

What do I think of when I hear the word sin?

Day 246

The Willingness to Offer the Gift

In the Christian eucharistic service, the bread and wine are brought to the altar by the people, and later the consecrated food comes back from the altar to those who first brought it forward. The movement is good: Whatever we are willing to hand over is returned to us as the Eternal Christ. "Whatever is offered for Incarnation is thereby redeemed," said some early church fathers.

Any parent understands. When your children bring forward their scribbles and drawings, you smile with delight and put them on the refrigerator for all to see! The child brims with satisfaction and pride. Of course, it is not Van Gogh, but that doesn't matter. It was not the perfection of the gift, but the willingness and desire of Johnny to give the gift that made you happy and made it a truly "sacramental" moment. It's the same with God. We deny ourselves sacraments every day by insisting on strange and impossible kinds of perfection and magic.

How do I picture myself in this ultimate reality of God? Can I imagine myself connected always and held always in this endless love?

Day 247

The Sacred Wound

You *will* be wounded. Your work is to find God and grace inside the wounds. This is why Jesus told Thomas, "Put your finger here and see my hands. Reach out your hand and put it in my side" (John 20:27). Thomas was trying to resolve the situation mentally, as men usually do, so Jesus had to force direct physical contact with human pain—the pain of Jesus, Thomas's capacity for empathy with that pain, and very likely with Thomas's own denied pain. Deep healing has to happen corporeally and emotionally, and not just abstractly.

Jesus wanted Thomas to face and feel in his body *the tragedy of it all—and then know it was not tragedy at all!* In that order. That is how wounds become sacred wounds. This is the pattern of all authentic conversion in the Christian economy of grace: not around, not under, not over, but *through* the wound we are healed and saved.

What wound do I have now, and am I allowing it to make me wise?

DAY 248

LEARNING TO DEAL WITH LIFE'S WOUNDS

Later in life, the man who has gone through initiation as a boy can recall his wounding, and its memory will help him move through and integrate the other inevitable wounds and defeats of life. He remembers that he is part of a bigger story and that he is not alone, nor the first to encounter hardship.

Today, because we don't dramatically and consciously move through any initiation, our wounds do not lead us to any bigger story. Without such sacraments, we just complain, get depressed, and lose all sacred perspective. The price we pay for this in terms of neuroses, anger, and litigation might just destroy modern secular culture from within.

We must learn, early and often, that wounds can produce wisdom, if we receive them as teachers.

How have I been taught to deal with my wounds?

Day 249

Life Is Not Just

Life is not just. Whether you are good or bad, there is no recipe for constant success in life, no formula to ensure that everything will work in your favor. We don't do ourselves or anybody else a favor by claiming that we can demand or expect perfect fairness—*which does not mean we should not work for it!*

Those who are poor and excluded learn this much earlier. They might be fatalistic, but they're also realistic, which can enable them to be happy in a way wealthy people are not. That's why Jesus said, "Blessed are you who are poor" (Luke 6:20). Life has given them an understanding and acceptance of the essentially tragic nature of human life. The rest of us, usually with a false sense of entitlement, have to learn it the hard way, if we learn it at all. It also makes comfortable people often unhappy, angry, or irritable when they cannot control every contingency.

When did I first understand that life is not fair?

Day 250

Justice and the Gospel

Social justice lies at the very "hearability" of the gospel message. Many of us don't understand the Bible's bias, because so few of us come from a situation of persecution. Middle-class white men living inside an empire don't hear Jesus' words as do people coming out of poverty, oppression, enslavement, and marginalization—as did Jesus' first hearers.

According to the Jewish prophets, and Jesus himself, persecution is *the privileged spiritual perspective for any teachable people*. Jesus said, "Blessed are you when people revile you and persecute you and utter all kinds of evil against you falsely on my account" (Matthew 5:11). The first people to hear the gospel and respond to it knew their need and emptiness, and their desire for real liberation. The notion of "salvation" was not yet spiritualized. We must find the rejected and fearful parts within ourselves, or, even better, we must befriend at least one person outside of our success system—or we will never have the privileged perspective of the gospel.

When am I most likely to recognize how needy I really am? How can I get to that place willingly?

Day 251

Social Sin

Social sin is difficult for us to understand because we haven't been trained to recognize our complicity in institutional evil, what Pope John Paul II called "structural sin." It's easier to obsess over and confess a few dirty thoughts or be impatient with my wife—and be done with it. In the first two thousand years of Christianity, our preaching concern has targeted primarily private sin, not social sin. We are finally beginning to understand that people do harmful things because they are part of sinful systems, cultures, and institutions.

We can remain nice Christians as long as we deal only with effects or symptoms. We don't question the system as long as we simply heal people and offer consolation. Mainline Christianity usually prefers charity to justice. In fact, if you want to guarantee a low turnout for a lecture in many Christian churches, just put the word "justice" in the title.

Where can I identify the structural sin in my personal world of family, work, church, and community?

Day 252

Mirror Neurons

One way to break free from our illusions as privileged men is to develop empathy for the rest of the world. We ask God to allow us to suffer emotionally, in our bodies and not just in our minds, what it feels like to be powerless, neglected, oppressed, or excluded.

If a child receives loving mirroring from mother and father, he develops more "mirror neurons" in brain and body and can more easily empathize with others. Some people cannot feel other peoples' suffering, a condition which, at its worst, produces the sociopathic or psychopathic personality.

If you did not get that mirroring as a child, and you don't relate easily to others' pain, I urge you to build the daily practice of looking at Jesus on the cross. Maybe we can still develop some mirror neurons later in life. As the prophet Zechariah proclaimed: "When they look on the one whom they have pierced, they shall mourn for him, as one mourns for an only child, and weep bitterly over him, as one weeps over a firstborn" (12:10).

What can I do to stand under the truth of what the world suffers?

Day 253

The Line between Joy and Suffering

In the Christian tradition, the more deeply we enter the mystery of Christ, the thinner the line becomes between joy and suffering, between tears of happiness and tears of sadness. There is only one concern for the man who gives his heart to God: "Am I doing God's will?" (i.e., "Am I helping God's people?")

Whether the answer brings us immediate happiness or immediate sadness is no longer of primary importance. It is a paradox of our faith that we feel joy when we can meaningfully suffer for or with others, not when we avoid it. And we feel sadness when we turn away from the pain of others, not when we unite with it.

What has suffering accomplished
in my soul lately?

DAY 254

ONLY LOVE AND GRACE

Authentic transformation is never achieved by laying guilt and shame on people; doing so only paralyzes them, or creates "push-back" and passive-aggressive behavior. It is amazing to me as a priest of forty years that the church does not know that. God knows it, however, and motivates humans in a much more positive way that elicits no push-back whatsoever.

People use guilt and shame all the time to make others compliant (even some clergy operate like policemen), but such forced compliance does not effect change for long, or at all, because the soul remains virtually untouched. *Only love and grace touch the soul, not fear, guilt, or shame.* Fear, guilt, shame, and coercion are the flimsy tools of the ego against the ego—and only to the ego-driven personality do they make any sense.

How have shame and guilt been used on me to force compliance—or how have I used shame and guilt on others?

Day 255

This Imperfect World

On the spiritual path, it is not optional to know ourselves. It's not optional to be willing to make a mistake. Such qualities are essential. They lead to the gradual growth of a man "to maturity, to the measure of the full stature of Christ" (Ephesians 4:13). The reason we sin and suffer is not because we are weak or wrong but simply because we are human. In this school sin abounds, but grace abounds even more (Romans 5:21) to have the final say. Remember, *God uses evil for God's own purposes.* God uses imperfection to achieve God's true kind of perfection; God uses weakness to create strength (2 Corinthians 12:10); God uses humans to create sons and daughters of God.

Being human means to be imperfect, to be limited, and thus to change and travel on a perpetual journey. Mature spirituality gives us the ability to live joyfully in an imperfect world. This is important because an imperfect world is the only one we have. And if God does not love imperfect people, God has no one to love.

How do I react to my own mistakes? What frustrates me most about being human and not perfect?

Day 256

Submarines

Mistakes aren't terrible in and of themselves; the problems come if we don't grow up because of them. If you're making the same mistakes at fifty that you made at twenty, something's wrong. You are expected to make them at twenty, but that's why you need guides, mentors, impulse control, and father figures.

One reason we repeat mistakes is that we were never allowed to develop our own inner authority, usually by a process of trial and error and bearing the consequences of our actions. Observing, naming, and owning our behavior patterns slowly creates a calm inner authority; we call this maturity.

Structures based on outer authority, enforcement, and punishment create men who can become expert at pretending, hiding, and denying. In such systems compliance, not self-awareness, is the goal. The true self goes underground and then comes out in unhealthy and disguised ways years later. We call these behaviors "submarines." Ask anyone who has been in jail, the military, a boarding school, or even a seminary.

Can I identify mistakes I'm making now that I made years ago? Can I name the patterns in my life that help me deny mistakes rather than name them?

DAY 257

THISNESS

We must not plunder with mere concepts and abstractions what is the unique mystery of each act of God. As Blessed John Duns Scotus taught us Franciscans, God creates *only* individuals. Universals and categories exist only in words and the mind. Each thing that exists, exists in its "thisness," and God maintains each and every thing in creation by an "immediate sustaining attentiveness" in its uniqueness.

No surprise that the Jesuit poet Gerard Manley Hopkins and the American prophet Thomas Merton considered themselves Scotists. Hopkins gives the best poetic description of "thisness" that I can imagine, in the following excerpt from "As Kingfishers Catch Fire":

Each mortal thing does one thing and the same:
Deals out that being indoors each one dwells;
Selves—goes itself; *myself* it speaks and spells,
Crying *What I do is me: for that I came*.
I say . . .
Acts in God's eye what in God's eye he is—
Christ—for Christ plays in ten thousand places,
Lovely in limbs, and lovely in eyes not his
To the Father through the features of men's faces.

How do I use generalizations to belittle what God is doing in me or someone else?

Day 258

No Easy Answers

Part of being an adult is a man's ability to trust himself. He looks with wiser vision on the mistakes he's made, the wrong turns, the false starts, and a hundred other small and large defeats he's suffered. If he can accept himself and claim all that he's learned from what he's done well—and not so well—he begins to understand that there are no easy answers. Most scholars in the field are agreeing that we move from very dualistic thinking when we are young to increasingly nondual thinking as we mature—from the mere knowledge of facts and information to the synthesis called wisdom.

God often refuses to give us answers. Maybe God knows there is no one right answer; God also knows he will make good even our mistakes. Instead of giving answers, God calls us to communion.

What do I really want from God—easy answers or the knowledge that God is happy that I exist?

Day 259

The Greatest Paradox

Perhaps the greatest paradox of the spiritual journey is this: wisdom and love do not come from success but from continuing failure. As St. Paul said, "When I am weak is when I am strong."

Our seeming negative balance becomes the very emptiness that God loves to fill, if only we will allow it. Our poverty keeps us seeking, desiring, trusting, hoping, and longing for God. It allows us to know without any doubt that God is doing all the giving, and we are always the receivers, even though we offer our sincere but limited response now and then.

I promise you that God rushes to fill any emptiness, longing, or desire that we offer. If you offer your completeness, God knows it is not true. Jesus seems to make this point in the shocking story of the tax collector and the Pharisee (Luke 18:10): the Pharisee offers his actual rightness and is deemed wrong by Jesus; the tax collector offers his actual wrongness and is deemed right by Jesus. This is rather amazing by every standard of organized religion.

Among those who know me, what authority have
I gained from my failures and suffering?

Day 260

Seeing

A spiritual man will always be lead to some form of prayer, meditation, or contemplation—what the great traditions might call *wisdom seeing*. Without it, he will not significantly change his "hard drive." This kind of seeing allows us to be happy and alone, and also happy with others. It allows people to be comfortable with paradox and mystery, connected to human suffering, yet largely immune to the influence of mass consciousness and its silly promises. These are really different people, and not just people who have a few loyalty symbols. They seem to live in a different world that both deeply connects them with other peoples' worlds, and yet also leaves them positively detached and content.

Thus, prayer is not a pious exercise that you do now and then to please God. It is an entirely alternative consciousness, created by the Spirit breathing and loving and desiring in you and through you, and often in spite of you! It ends up creating an entirely different set of eyes in a person, and surely a different heart for everything.

As I look back over the past ten years, where has the true religion happened in my life?

Day 261

Father of the Faith

The man who accepts the conventions of climbing the career ladder, who buys into the myths of success, money, and power, becomes a tragic hero in a culture of conformity. This usually happens to men between the ages of twenty and thirty-five, when they are busy doing what their culture tells them they're supposed to be doing. Most men at this stage don't really know who they are. *They just know who they are supposed to be and what they are supposed to do.* Meeting expectations can become a trap from which a man will spend the rest of his life trying to escape.

Abraham gave up his lands, family, wealth, and reputation: "Go from your country and your kindred and your father's house to the land that I will show you" (Genesis 12:1). He responded to the subversive voice of God that would make no sense to an American man today. Three of the world's great religions call Abraham the father of their faith, but most of the faithful don't agree with his path at all.

Am I still doing what other voices (besides God's) are telling me I should be doing—or have I begun a journey similar to Abraham's?

Day 262

Process, Not Outcome

To understand the subversive nature of the spiritual call of God, let's look at Abraham again. He moved from security to insecurity, from having all the answers to having no answers. He left everything behind to follow what the divine voice had commanded. He was promised sons as numerous as the sands beside the sea and the stars of the heavens.

But Abraham died before he saw that promise fulfilled. I wonder if he ever said that things hadn't panned out? Did he consider himself a fool or a failure? He put his hope and identity in a different kind of success. Abraham trusted the journey itself, not simply the promised destination. Today, we might say that Abraham trusted the process more than the outcome. Faith is a method for enlightenment now much more than a requirement for going to heaven later.

How comfortable am I with the possibility that I die before receiving the rewards I'm seeking?

Day 263

Sweat Lodge

Sometimes the only way out of our self-pity and preoccupation with hard-to-shake feelings is to realize our connection with a vast history, with others on the earth now, and with a long evolutionary future. These are times to seek solidarity with men and women who suffer now, who will suffer, and who have suffered before us. I've made several sweat lodges with Native Americans. Twenty-eight hot rocks are brought in, symbolizing the days of a woman's cycle, and in the dark steam, we pray in naked discomfort for our ancestors before us, for those living now, and for the children and grandchildren yet to come. It is like sacraments of water baptism, brutally honest confession, and intimate communion with brothers all at once! Men respect it, because they cannot fake it. On many reservations, it is by far the most successful form of recovery from all addictions. The church has much to learn from Native peoples, like what sacraments really are.

Can I name specific people with whom I share suffering and whose suffering I share?

DAY 264

CHANGE VERSUS TRANSFORMATION

There's a difference between change and transformation. Change happens when something old dies and something new begins. *Transformation happens when we personally change in the process of outer change.* Did you know that planned change is even more troublesome to the ego than unplanned change? Just watch how we love to hate all authorities who legislate for us. The ego wants to find a way to avoid changing if at all possible, but most especially if another ego is commanding it.

God usually has to demand change of us. In fact, we call some unavoidable changes "acts of God," and those often elicit actual transformation more than anything else. If anybody is asking us to change—be it our partner, Congress, the church, the neighborhood association—every form of ego control and resistance will come out to accuse, defend, shout, and oppose. Jean Vanier told me many years ago that I should assume most Western people have two wounds: one in their sexuality and the other in their relationship to authority. I have found this to be true.

What was the last change I fought tooth and nail?

Day 265

Liberation from the Hall of Mirrors

Conversion could be described as a process of becoming increasingly disenchanted with our small, separate self and recognizing how afraid and needy it is. The only way to break free of the fear and insecurity is to sever our attachment to (1) who we *think* we are, (2) who we need to be, and (3) who others want us to be. These form a hall of distorted mirrors, illuminating nothing.

The best way out is to find one true Mirror, who illuminates you with understanding, showing you why you do the things you do the way you do them. *The One who understands all can forgive all, which is why forgiveness is God's business.* As St. Francis of Assisi said, "I am who I am in God's eyes—nothing more, but nothing less either."

What is my present level of fear? Of insecurity?
What does that fear or insecurity indicate about
the attachments in my life?

Day 266

You Already Know

The best thing we can do as teachers, believers, friends, parents, and lovers is to help people recognize and trust their *spiritual intuitions*. That deeper place is what Christians call the indwelling presence of the Holy Spirit (Romans 5:5), always crying out "Abba," or "Papa" (Galatians 4:4–7), which is a child's trustful name for his daddy. That inner voice already knows the truth (1 John 2:21), that you are both a son and an heir of God! We wait and hope for someone to confirm this intuition, because it seems too good to be true.

God plants the truth within each person, and then our job is to confirm it for one another. We are never left alone; God offers real guidance and the core truth from within—if we could but trust it. Too much emphasis on outer church authority tends to make people discount and mistrust this deepest and truest inner voice, which is always crying "Abba."

When have I mistrusted my deeper intuition?
When have I trusted that intuition
so far as to act on it?

Day 267

Country Club Religion

Early-stage religion is more about belonging and believing than about transformation. When belonging and believing are the primary concerns, people don't see their need for growth, healing, or basic spiritual curiosity. Once we let the group substitute for an inner life or our own faith journey, all we need to do is "attend." For several centuries, *church has been more a matter of attendance at a service than an observably different lifestyle.* Membership requirements and penalties predominated, not the change-your-life message that Jesus so clearly preached.

Membership questions lead to endless arguments about who is in and who is out, who is right and who is wrong, who is worthy of our God, and who is not. Such distinctions appeal to our ego and its need to feel worthy and superior and to be a part of a group that defines itself by exclusion. The church ends up a gated country club, giving people a false sense of superiority. This is why Jesus walks to those on the edges: the handicapped, the sinners, the excluded ones.

How much of my life is a matter of attendance to a specific group of people? How much of my life is a process of real change within?

Day 268

Mind Your Own Business

We want guidance and leadership from people who can say, "I know what God does with pain. I should be blaming or bitter, but because of God and grace, I'm not." We long for real people who are practiced in transforming pain, as Jesus did on the cross. These are the only spiritual authorities worth following. The rest of us just talk.

Such true spiritual authority does not simply say, "You must believe in this," or "This formula will get you to heaven," or "I know who God approves of," as if that is anyone's business but God's. Only the small ego-self would ask such superiority questions; the true soul is bored and bothered by them.

I remember the Sisters of Charity who taught me as a boy in Kansas, who often said that the eleventh commandment in the classroom was "MYOB," or "mind your own business"! We need mountains of growth, grace, and conversion ourselves without trying to make decisions for God or for others.

When have I tried to butt into God's business?

Day 269

Junk Religion

Jesus and the Buddha made it clear to their followers that *life is suffering, and we cannot avoid it.* Every person carries pain—it's in a big black bag that gets heavier as we get older, filled with betrayals, rejections, disappointments, and hurts inflicted along the way. We'd better know what to do with all of this, because it will not just go away. Women tend to talk about it, which can turn it into gossip or lead to healing. Men are more likely to stuff their pain—or export it to Iraq or wherever today's enemy resides.

If we don't find a way to transform our pain, we will *always* transmit it to those around us or turn it against ourselves. And we'll create tension, negativity, suspicion, and fear wherever we go. Anyone who encourages you to project your pain onto others (Muslims, your family, gays, etc.) or to turn it against yourself has no truth or wisdom to offer. If your religion is not teaching you how to recognize, hold, and transform suffering, it is junk religion.

Do I transform my pain or transmit it?

Day 270

What Good Is Suffering?

Suffering is our necessary perception of evil. If we don't feel evil, we stand apart from it, numb and aloof, and do not see our own complicity in it. Jesus did not numb himself or stand above pain; in fact the cross reveals his utter solidarity with all the suffering of history. It was God's way of joining us at our lowest moments. I'm not sure how or why, but our suffering unites us to God and to other people—and therefore to ourselves.

The irony is not that God should feel so fiercely but that God's creatures should feel so feebly. If you find nothing to cry about or no injustice that deserves your anger, then you are blind and out of touch. We need to make personal the immense pain of humanity, of animals, of the earth itself, which is all the very pain of God. He holds it first, we hold it second. If we agree to hold it with him, I think we actually participate in the salvation of the world (See Colossians 1:24–25).

What suffering can I identify and name
in my life right now?

Day 271

From Whistling to Believing

For some men, faith is a form of whistling in the dark, hoping against hope that God is as good as advertised. But when we're honest with ourselves, we doubt whether God is really on our side, or even good. But the desire itself, the desire to believe, is a healthy starting place. Just trust the desire.

This initial impulse toward future faith is already the work of grace in your life and not to be dismissed easily. This is the point at which many men begin the spiritual path to real faith. Today, you may be simply whistling in the dark and hoping; tomorrow, you may be there, still wondering how you got there. It is never a rational process, but neither is it irrational. It is "trans-rational." God plants in you the desire for what God wants to give you, you somehow agree, and it eventually happens. You think you are doing it, but you know you didn't—and that somehow it was done to you!

How would I describe my faith?

DAY 272

HABAKKUK'S HAIR

There's a Jewish legend about a lesser-known prophet with the strange name of Habakkuk. He is busy making a stew for himself, with no time to hear God's call to go feed Daniel in the lion's den (14:31–42), so an angel of Yahweh has to pick him up by the hair and take him there with stew in hand. After Daniel eats, the text says that the angel "lost no time in returning Habakkuk back home." It seems he was a rather lazy and reluctant prophet.

Many times in my life when I find myself in a new place spiritually, and I know I had little to do with it, I feel I have been taken and returned like old Habakkuk. But as I get balder, I think the angel must have a harder time getting me up and down.

When has God picked me up and carried me somewhere else?

Day 273

Pictures Do It!

The psychologist Carl Jung said that deep transformation happens primarily in the presence of images. They alone can touch the unconscious—in one invasive and healing reconfiguration of the soul. It might also take the form of a biography, a song, a theater piece, a movie, a dream image, a sculpture, an inner vision, a piece of art. But after the encounter, you see things differently. One hundred sermons could never have moved you to this new place.

Ideas and concepts don't change people; they tend to keep us inside our dualistic thinking, judging back and forth whether we agree with the idea, the wording, who said it, or how he said it. One could say that the reason we have 30,000 Christian denominations in the world now, is that they made it all depend on words. They should have known that "the Word became flesh."

But here am I, a supposedly Catholic boy, writing more and more words! None of them will "take" until they become an image inside you.

What images fascinate me, call to me? What are they saying?

Day 274

Larger-Than-Life Men

We describe some people as larger than life. If we could see their history, we would learn that at some point they were led to the edge of their own resources and found the actual Source. They suffered a breakdown, which felt like dying. But instead of breaking down, they broke through! Instead of avoiding, shortchanging, or raging against death, they went through death—a death to their old self, their small life, their imperfections, their illusory dreams, their wounds, their grudges, and their limited sense of their own destiny.

When they did this, they came out on the other side knowing that death henceforth could do them no harm. "What did I ever lose by dying?" they say. This process is supposed to be the baptismal initiation rite into Christianity, where we first "join him in the tomb" and then afterwards "join him in his resurrection" (Romans 5:4–5). We are all supposed to be larger-than-death men, appearing to the world as larger than life. This should be the definition of a Christian man.

What death have I experienced in myself, and what happened as a result?

Day 275

Weight Lifting

St. Paul says that there's a kind of weight to the evil and sorrow we carry; he also refers to glory having weight. "An eternal weight of glory beyond all measure" is going to be shown to us (2 Corinthians 4:17). I believe both weights are too heavy for one person to carry. It's a corporate mystery we are part of. God is saving the world (John 4:42) and not just private souls. The Bible is a salvation history, not a private itinerary.

Paul also speaks of the "body of death" and the "body of resurrection" almost as if it's a huge force field that we live inside of, and Jesus is the front man for it all. He's our "corporate personality" holding us inside the mystery of transformation. We are the willing (or unwilling) participants in this great cosmic reality. Our conscious yes allows us to participate in carrying the weight of sorrow, along with the weight of glory. We cannot do it alone but only together "in Christ," which is by far Paul's single most common phrase.

When have I experienced the weight of glory?

Day 276

Day-to-Day Gratitude

Things go right more often than they go wrong. Our legs carry us where we are going, our eyes let us see the road ahead, and our ears let us hear the world around us. Our bodies, and our lives, work pretty much as they should, which is why we become so unsettled when we confront any failure or injustice. This is not so true for people born into intense poverty or social injustice, of course. And we had best never forget that.

Nevertheless, we must stop a moment and look clearly and honestly at our life thus far. For most of us, life has been pretty good.

We shouldn't be naïve about evil, but perhaps the most appropriate attitude on a day-to-day basis should be *simple and overwhelming gratitude for what has been given*. From that overflowing abundance will come the energy to work for those who have a life of scarcity and sadness.

For what am I grateful, in the midst of my full and complex life?

DAY 277

LETTING GO

For most of human history, the great inner journey was taught in sacred space and ritual form at key moments of transitioning. This clarified, distilled, and shortened the process. The task was very clear, and it was about letting go in one form or another. It was not a lecture series or a lifetime of weekend retreats, or even church services.

Because rites of passage and sacred space have fallen out of favor in our consumer culture, most people don't learn how to move past their fear of diminishment, even when it stares them down or gently invites them inward and onward. They are not "prepared [for] the Passover" (Mark 14:16), as it were. This lack of preparation for the Passover—our lack of training in grief work, our not knowing how to let go of small life, and our failure to entrust ourselves to a much bigger life—sets the stage for one spiritual crisis after another.

All great spirituality is about letting go. God takes care of filling us up.

What grief work am I doing now?
What have I had to let go?

Day 278

A Little Like Dying

When you have spent your whole life protecting and polishing your hard-won identity in this world, it will surely feel like dying to let go of it. In fact, it is an absurd notion. And until you are fully at home in your new digs, you will think of a hundred good reasons to run back to the old run-down apartment. We are rather total victims of the familiar and the habitual, if we do not actively practice dying and moving on.

Every movement toward union with God will be experienced as a loss of self-importance and a loss of self-control as we slowly release control to Another. It will always be a loss of the familiar, but we'll come to see how small was the comfort provided by the familiar. We are being invited into purpose, significance, and comfort that are much broader and deeper. But we won't know that until we have been in that new place for a while.

When have I felt as if I were dying
to an old way of life?

Day 279

Old Fools

M any of us grow more rigid and opinionated as we age. We're supposed to move from the dualistic thinking of ten-year-old boys to the nondual mind of wise mentors. We're supposed to move from either/or to both/and thinking as we grow up. This is why, all things being equal, elders should be better at patience, forgiveness, mercy, and compassion than teenagers.

But if we remain self-assured, self-righteous, self-seeking, dualistic thinkers, and left-brained at that, we cannot become bridge builders or agents of reconciliation—not even in our own families or neighborhoods.

Presently, our religious leaders seem uninterested in true interfaith dialogue. Our politicians seem capable not of seeking the common good but only of working with win/lose models. Those at the helm of the financial sector live on extravagant bonuses, while much of the world goes hungry. Instead of moving away from dualistic thinking, the people who could have become mentors have instead used the system to become even more entrenched and dualistic!

The result: we have moved backward, and our society has grown more infantile.

What opportunities do I have to move toward a
wise mentor mentality?

Day 280

Two Must Give Way to Something New

"He has abolished the law with its commandments and ordinances, that he might create in himself one new humanity in place of the two, thus making peace, and might reconcile both groups to God in one body through the cross" (Ephesians 2:15–16).

Those of us in positions of power, education, or authority must liberate the weak and oppressed from injustice and pass on the many benefits that we enjoy in our "developed" world. The weak and the poor must liberate us from our illusions and our innocence. They also must offer us some alternative worldview to mere capitalism, entertainment, and self-advancement.

Sometimes I think that the two genders, the division of East and West, the two hemispheres of the brain, the political divisions of liberal and conservative, the light-skinned and the dark-skinned—all must give way to something new and much better. Neither side of any issue is going to concede or disappear. If we don't acknowledge the reality of the body of Christ, beloved of God, we will lose the ability to imagine ourselves—or others—as whole.

**Whom do I have trouble imagining as wonderful
and loved by God?**

DAY 281

CRUCIFIXION AND RESURRECTION

Resurrection without crucifixion is only half the truth. Crucifixion without resurrection is only half the truth.

They are forever wrapped inside of one eternal and fruitful Whole.

If we try to have one without the other, we destroy the big mystery.

How have I experienced both crucifixion and resurrection?

Day 282

Spirit and Spirits

C an it be an accident that in some languages the word "spirits" is used to describe alcohol? Why would we dignify something that can cause so much pain by calling it "spirit"?

Remember that in the work of transformation, the wound is often the place of breakthrough. The place of the pain is the place of the promise. *Salvation is sin turned around.* We even use fermented wine as the Sacrament of the Eucharist! The supposed worst becomes for us the very best.

What does alcohol do to the body? It intoxicates, it takes us beyond the rational, and it risks destroying us. An authentic experience of God has some of the same characteristics. Our mystics, almost without exception, have spoken of God as an intoxicating and ecstatic lover. God-experience can be dangerous, tempting us to think too highly of ourselves. Immature people can become addicted to God-talk and misuse it for their own purposes. An experience of God is also trans-rational and usually requires that we relinquish control.

Yes, the Spirit is intoxicating—in the best possible way.

What God-experiences do I especially remember, and why?

DAY 283

WHAT IS SOUL WORK?

Most Christians think of the soul as the eternal part of a person that goes to heaven or to hell. But that's not the historic meaning of soul, even as Jesus would have understood it. Soul had to do with depth. If spirit is our striving upward for the divine, then soul is the part of us that goes down to the depths of things, into meaning, the unconscious, the deeper truth, and the symbolic. The soul works with dreams, music, story, and poetry. It is our interior blueprint, our divine DNA, and our true self.

Too often we have encouraged people to fly up to Spirit before descending into soul. Such people seek height without depth, answers without honest questions, God without self, heaven without earth, and religion without embodiment. This has not been good for the gospel. Remember, the goal and promise at the end of the Bible is "a new heaven and a new earth" (Revelation 21:1), and not heaven disconnected from earth. Even in the creed, Jesus "descended into hell" before he "ascended into heaven."

What is my experience of moving
into the depths of things?

DAY 284

BLOOD

In men's spirituality, few symbols are more potent than blood. Blood is ubiquitous in spirituality and mythology. Apparently in the female psyche, blood is associated with life because of menstruation and labor. For men, it relates mostly to death, because we associate it with dying on battlefields. No wonder so many Christians spoke commonly of the blood of Christ, the precious blood, and being saved by the blood, imagined as a flowing life force moving toward us.

Life doesn't get real until it somehow draws blood, as it were. Death is not real till blood is in sight. Thus spiritual language is fascinated by both blood and the sword. It is when the sword pierces the heart and blood is shed that the profound insights are revealed and we begin to encounter big truth and true self. Apparently, they are trying to say, the price for these is very high. Imagine the price for touching God!

What images and feelings arise in me when
I see or think about blood?

Day 285

Drink This

In initiation rites, the young man was often circumcised so he would become more familiar with the price of blood. He was told that the woman has to bleed to give new life, and now he must also bleed and suffer in that generative member that he most associates with pleasure, power, and male prowess. The woman doesn't need to make the intellectual connection between bloodletting and new life; she learns it naturally on a bodily level.

One wonders if Christians who drink the "blood of Christ" at the Eucharist have any idea that they're participating in a form of ancient initiation, where the young boys drank the blood of their fathers and elders to know who they were. Henceforth, they had no doubt whose blood was in their veins. Thus Jesus did not say, "Think about this," or "Look at this," or even "Adore this." He said "Drink this!"

If I consider that the Eucharist is a way to take into myself the essence of Jesus, how might that affect the way I go about my life?

Day 286

The Big Turnaround

Throughout religion's history, humans had to spill blood to access God. It started with human sacrifice, moved to animal sacrifice, and then to various forms of self-denial and personal sacrifice lasting into our own time. People couldn't imagine making contact with a transcendent and distant God without spilling blood. The sad effect was that God lodged in the human psyche as a tyrant and not a lover, one we feared and tried to placate, not one who loved us.

Consider now the story of Jesus. God/Jesus spills blood *to get to us*—rather than demanding our blood to get to God. This is what the writer of the Letter to the Hebrews meant by one and final sacrifice. The eternal flow of life from God to humanity is offered through the body of Jesus (Hebrews 10:20), and the system of religious sacrifice, now unnecessary, is finished. God yearns for us, God spills the blood from God's side, Jesus opens the heart of God toward us, and blood and water flow out (John 19:34). God lives and dies for the beloved creation.

What does it mean to me that God no longer requires a sacrifice?

Day 287

"Born Again" Implies Dying First

Who of us wants to die? I would rather admire Jesus than follow him to Calvary. We are like the first apostles, who opposed him every step of the way. But Jesus was clear: "Unless a grain of wheat falls into the earth and dies, it remains just a single grain" (John 12:24). We have now found this same line in ancient initiation rites.

So, if a spiritual leader tells you that you can be born again or achieve some kind of salvation but does not first speak to you frankly about dying or letting go of your life in a major way, then just keep on walking.

In all of creation, no new birth occurs without a preceding loss. Death and new life are in an eternal embrace. The cleverest way by which we've avoided following Jesus on his path toward death was to worship him. He never once said, "Worship me," but he clearly said, "Follow me" a number of times—and we know where he was headed.

What is coming to an end in my life? What do I sense is being born?

Day 288

Paradox and the Contemplative Mind

Great religion is full of paradoxes. A paradox is something that appears to be contradictory, but if seen from another angle or with a different mind, is not a contradiction at all but a deep truth. We Catholics love paradoxes: Jesus is fully human yet fully divine. Mary is virgin and yet mother. The Eucharist is bread and Jesus at the same time. God is three and one at the same time. These are logical contradictions and cannot be processed with a dualistic mind. To deal with spirituality, you need different software, which I call contemplation or nondual consciousness. Paul simply called it understanding spiritual things spiritually (1 Corinthians 2:6–16).

Once we stopped teaching the contemplative mind, we set up the Western world for rationalism and secularism. We lost our unique access point, our "new mind" and alternative consciousness. We told Christians to keep believing these doctrines, which always were paradoxes, but we no longer gave them the proper software with which to understand them. Is it any surprise that atheism emerged primarily in the Christian West?

How do I normally deal with paradox?

DAY 289

TIME TO GROW UP

"When I was a child, I thought like a child; when I became an adult, I put an end to childish ways" (1 Corinthians 13:11).

Many middle-aged Catholic men who go to confession say exactly the same things they confessed at the age of twenty, according to many of us who have inquired. They have not grown more sophisticated in their self-understanding—or in their understanding of God, for that matter. Childhood conditioning still reigns.

How is it that so many of us obtained major education and experience in our fields of interest, but we hang on to infantile notions of God, sin, salvation, forgiveness, church, and love? Our work at MALEs is trying to create adult religion and adult men, men who can be partners to their wives, fathers to their children, intelligent and nonreactionary citizens, and servants of God in this suffering world.

How has my understanding of myself changed over the years, if at all? How has my understanding of God changed, or has it?

Day 290
Grown-Up Faith

If we're on the path of transformation, we should become more nuanced and subtle as we grow older. We learn how to recognize our own demons. We don't let them fool us anymore about what's going on. We also learn to trust our own angels, and allow them to lead, and heal, and guide. Inner experience and inner authority begin to balance out an exclusive reliance upon what the pope or Bible says. God does not want robots, but free and conscious lovers.

How has my faith changed from when
I was a boy?

Day 291

Men and Nature

Did you ever notice that most of the major God-encounters of men in the Bible happened out in the natural world? Abraham on pilgrimage, Moses at the burning bush, David watching sheep, John the Baptist down at the river, Jesus in the desert for forty days, Amos trimming sycamore trees, Paul on the road to Damascus. They never seem to happen in temples, shrines, schools, or synagogues.

Nature is the only thing that men inherently respect; they know it is bigger and more powerful than they are. Inside the natural world, men are more likely to open up, weep, surrender, forgive, discover themselves, and know ecstatic joy. Out in nature is where a lot of men do their real praying.

Where have I encountered God?

Day 292

Nature Deficit Disorder

My spiritual father, St. Francis, was one of the few later Christian saints who made a consistent and clear connection with nature. Yet much of Christian history has had to do with books, translations, and universities; internecine fights among academics and seminaries; and people arguing about words, salvation theories, and worship styles.

We are suffering from a major case of Christian NDD— Nature Deficit Disorder. At this point, I sincerely believe that the earth is the only thing shared enough, wise enough, suffering enough, and God-created enough to truly change most men. Get out, stay quiet, be alone, and listen long and happily. "Nature is the primary and most perfect revelation of the divine," said St. Thomas Aquinas. It was the Bible before the Bible, and we stopped reading it.

How do I spend time with nature? How can I make that time more conducive to spiritual wonder?

DAY 293

TAKE THE TIME IT TAKES

Transformation doesn't happen on our timetable. Remember that Jesus "fasted forty days and forty nights, and afterwards he was famished" (Matthew 4:2). It takes a long time to recognize your true hunger. Without good spiritual guidance, you will run from all inner chaos and aimlessness. Yet, this is God's best invitation to you!

Without deliberate practices over time, nothing new is going to happen. I predict that in the coming years we will be moving from a mere belief-based religion, which asks almost nothing of you except vague intellectual assent, to a *practice-based religion*, where you can experience things and know things for yourself. No authorities to believe and no authorities to fight. *You* must take the responsibility for your spiritual journey.

Solitude, silence, spiritual reading, contemplative practice, walking meditation, days alone in nature, journaling, spiritual direction, men's support groups, volunteer work outside your comfort zone, educating yourself on at least one social issue in depth—these are places in which I see men change.

---

*How do I escape transformation or at least
distract myself from it?*

PART 5
Male Archetypes and the Integrated Man—King, Warrior, Magician, Lover

In the second half of life men need honesty and humility more than they need heroism.
—Richard Rohr

✦ Most mythology, sacred story, and even Scripture constellate around four primary energies/images that are found in men. These characteristics recur so constantly and consistently, that we now recognize they describe the four parts of the male soul: the king/father in his fullness, the boundary-protecting warrior, the wise magician/sage, and the "taste it all" lover.

✦ As these "Four Great Ones" gradually come together, regulating and balancing one another, a man becomes God's great work of art, a true king/father. (Probably why so many men love their grandpa!) The default position is the dictator, the tyrant, the power-hungry old man (Saul and Herod in the Scriptures). He is the dark king with power but no power.

✦ If you overdo one archetypal energy and neglect the others, this will not only unbalance you, but it will destroy you in the

long run. You need all four to fully balance out. Knowledge
of the four archetypes becomes a discernment of spirits and a
guide for tracking your own blind spots and overstatements.
Frankly, it becomes one way to spot your "sin."

✦ If you want to do some exciting Scripture study to see how
Jesus really is the "son of David," the new whole man, just
go through the four Gospels and see how he consistently
moves between all four male energies. You do not have to be
a Christian to see that the human Jesus is at the same time
a prophet-warrior, a gentle lover of life, an outstanding sage,
and one who walks with the calm authority of a father-king.

Day 294

We Are Loved into Loving

God loves us into becoming lovers by a noncoercive and nonpunitive style of bringing us up. God assists from within by loving us at ever deeper levels—and we become loving almost in spite of ourselves. God just rubs off on us—and isn't that what you want to do for your kids? Our only homework is life itself, with all of its suffering, desiring, sinning, learning, winning, and losing—many times. God demands that we forgive seventy times seven so that we can recognize that this is how God operates first and always.

Like any good parent, God is willing to secretly help us with our homework, and to give us an A for even a mustard seed of love, desire, or effort. What else would make you want to love even more? What else would make you into a lover? Surely not punishment.

In what ways, times, and places do I experience
God's nonpunitive love?

Day 295

We Two Being Whole—Are One!

The spiritually whole man seeks to integrate within himself both masculine and feminine qualities by the end of his life. This human balance and integration is exemplified in Jesus himself, who had a masculine body along with a very feminine soul, which operated together as one—which was Spirit!

Jesus was not macho or patriarchal by any cultural definition whatsoever. Take this as the lesson: male and female are most alike at their most mature levels; male and female are most different at their most immature levels. In Jesus we can hardly tell the difference!

---

*In what ways have I integrated
feminine qualities?*

Day 296

Jump

For the young man to succeed in the world he will listen to his ego-consciousness—but it tells him only what he needs for succeeding in his small world. He will spend the first half of life following the agenda of some crowd, even though he swears he's not doing that. He has not yet met his soul or the god who is really God.

Then, in the second half of life, the rules change on him, and the things that worked in the first half of life usually no longer work. He doesn't really solve his problems; he just outgrows them. Thomas Merton wrote of men who spend their life climbing to the top of the ladder only to find that it's leaning against the wrong wall—and furthermore, there's nothing up there! The truly difficult conversion or enlightenment for men in the second half of life is learning that the only point to having climbed to the top of the ladder is to jump off, and to find everything that matters already present at the so-called bottom.

Have I placed my ladder against the wrong wall?
What really matters to me now?

Day 297

The Wheel

In the second half of life we come to understand that there is a spiral character to the life we've been living. At times, we may forget the journey, lose track of our quest, and drown in daily details. Many great spiritual traditions call this "the inexorable wheel" of dying and rising. This is the human pattern of remembering and forgetting, momentarily living and then dying again, even though we swore we would never repeat this mistake. Everything that we are and everything we hold dear will get tossed about at the mercy of life's spinning wheel of fortunes.

We must hold fast to an underlying trust that when we need help along our path it will appear. This is the shape of our trust in God. Once you have met your own soul, you know that you are being guided. You are being led from within, and even the inexorable wheel of life is your teacher. It is the cycle of failure and renewal that slowly lowers you into the arms of a very safe God.

When have I experienced a sense of life
in circular motion?

Day 298

Fire or Frozen

Modern men need to guard against losing their erotic instinct. That instinct is not primarily about sex; Eros is the life energy, the life force. Days when we are not erotic are days when we just don't care, when we have no motivation, when we simply don't give a damn. On those days when we feel charged up and highly motivated, we are filled with Eros. Erotic men change the world by their passion, whether they're on fire about bee keeping or their sports team or their marriage.

Eros is life energy, as opposed to Thanatos, which is death energy. A good word for Eros is "juice"; with Eros we are "juiced"! When there's no Eros, we're dead, although we might be formally faithful, celibate, or law abiding. Thanatos is seldom condemned by religion, even though it is quite common and deadening. Eros is much more feared and denounced for its possible excesses. Yet only erotic men attract, invite, change, and enliven other people.

When have I been particularly alive to life?

Day 299

People Who Energize

Don't you love to be with people who give out energy rather than drain it from you? People who exude creativity, initiative, and are deeply engaged with the world? You can feel it when you are with them. You feel safe, enlivened, and energized in their presence. So you seek them out, just as the crowds sought out Jesus and people today seek out truly wise and whole women and men. Their spiritual authority is compelling and does not need any title, role, or vestment—it simply is. These people are the living core of the Body of Christ.

That doesn't mean they are perfect. In fact, most creative and alive people have known their share of struggles and mistakes, but gained their inner authority by cooperating with grace, strength, and mercy. They are lightbulb people. They give and take from the Unlimited Source.

Who are the sources of energy in my life? How can I spend time with them and learn from them?

Day 300

The Wisdom of Our Bodies

Women more naturally learn to be in touch with their bodies. Men tend to listen more to our minds. We learn to ignore the bumps and bruises and lessons of the body, and play through the pain. I am told that women's very vocabulary for inner states and feelings is five to one over men! Women have some advantage here; menstruation and childbirth have shown them that life can be painful, and they have to be in contact with their "within." In that way, women have come to know the mystery and power of the body.

Somehow we men must make the same movement down into the flesh, exactly as Jesus did in the Incarnation. I often wonder if that is not at the bottom of our sexual desire. Isn't it interesting that many if not most of the world mythologies associated sky with father and earth with mother? Jesus is invariably telling males to come "down" in one sense or another, and he is usually inviting women to come "up." Hopefully we meet in the middle.

How have I come to understand and accept that my body is holy and has wisdom to offer? When and how can I spend time listening to my body?

Day 301

What Should We Remember?

On the night before Jesus died he got down on his knees and washed his disciples' feet. This self-giving act bypassed the rational and went straight to the disciples' hearts. What prompted him to perform this act?

Some time before, a woman entered a room where men had gathered to eat. She got down on her knees and washed Jesus' feet with her tears and dried them with her hair. Imagine the courage it took for a woman to enter that room. Imagine the pure love that moved her to wash Jesus' feet with her tears. Jesus said: "Truly I tell you, wherever this good news is proclaimed in the whole world, what she has done will be told in remembrance of her" (Matthew 26:13). Can you hear the echoes of Jesus' later invitation, "Do this in remembrance of me"? Perhaps he learned the power of washing feet from his encounter with the woman. We participate in the communion supper in memory of Jesus, but will we wash one another's feet in memory of her?

In what areas of my life do I have a leadership role? As I lead in the spirit of Jesus, whose feet do I wash? Or has my leadership not developed in this way?

DAY 302

A MISSING SACRAMENT

The washing of the feet is wonderful body theology, yet this "sacrament" was largely dropped in the churches, although it has much more scriptural basis than many of the seven official sacraments. The body is one important source for knowing beyond what we learn rationally. Massage therapists will tell you that the body does not lie. Many of us carry childhood memories in our shoulders, belly, back, or heart, yet we try to heal them just by thinking about healing. Is it any surprise that Jesus usually healed people by physically touching them?

Until spiritual healings are also located in the body, usually we cannot change deeply or permanently. I am convinced that this is the foundational meaning of Jesus' constant physical healings of people. He touched them all the way through! Not just some new idea, or a mere medical cure, but a whole new person was set loose.

How in tune am I to the wisdom of my body?
What has changed in my life because I paid
attention to what my body was telling me?

DAY 303

THE BODY KNOWS

The Christian belief in the Incarnation is that God took on human flesh. Thus we should not neglect our bodies and rely only on the soul or spirit. Our soul and spirit speak to us through the body until they finally operate as one. Even in the creed, we say that we believe in "the resurrection of the body," and the final book of the Bible promises not just a new heaven but a "new earth" as well (Revelation 21:1). If we keep eliminating the physical from the work of salvation, we don't remain true to the Christ mystery.

We men need to overcome our doubt about the goodness and holiness of the physical world, and of our own bodies. This blessing from St. Paul says it well: "May the God of peace himself sanctify you entirely; and may your *spirit and soul and body* be kept sound and blameless at the coming of our Lord Jesus Christ. The one who calls you is faithful, and he will do this" (1 Thessalonians 5:23–24).

How do I engage in a prayer of gratitude for my body and all its functions and capabilities, from head to toe?

Day 304

How to Tell a Saint

A saint is someone who has faced the dark side of himself and is no longer shocked by it. Saints have met and confronted the enemy within and forgiven it, joining God who forgave it first.

Saints know their brokenness all the way through, which causes them to rely hourly and daily on the mercy of God. Saints do not need *to appear* to be anything. Appearances are just that. Saints have learned to be at home in their naked being, where God has met them and loved them at the deepest level of their ordinariness.

Who do I know who can acknowledge the shadow side of human nature without being shocked by it or becoming obsessed with it? What can I learn from that person's example?

Day 305

Beginning with This Generation

It becomes clear who the real male elders are *after* initiation. Rather than just having another personal growth experience, such men realize they are merely a part of the cycle of generations. A truly initiated man realizes that life is not about him, but he is about the flow of life itself. He has *been taken care of* at the foundational level, and now he must care for others.

If it was a true initiation, no matter how it happened, a man will always move into larger worlds. He will return to his family, neighborhood, country, and church—with a gift. And *his larger self is the primary gift.* A truly initiated man knows that his task is to become "generative"—to help others, to protect the planet and all life around him. Like the Iroquois elders who made decisions not just for themselves but "for seven generations." This is authentic king energy. And we surely need some kings today at every level of church and society.

Who are the kings I have known? What impact have they had on my life and the lives of other men and boys around me?

Day 306

Those Who Fear Death

We won't be prepared to die until we have truly lived. For some paradoxical reason, people who have experienced life intensely and fully are the ones who are most able to let go of it. They seem to die with the same passion with which they lived. Those who most fear death are those who have not yet begun to live. Someone with a full life has learned already how to include death, and so death is not a stranger.

People with unlived lives unconsciously know that true insight and vitality have somehow eluded them, which leaves them without a center or even a sense of why they were ever born. Their real self—soul—has not been awakened, and so they lack a deep sense of themselves, or any eternal purpose. Having not yet begun to live, they can't imagine dying. It is still foreign territory, a destination preceded by no journey toward it. Anxiety haunts their nights and days, searching in outer places for what they can only find within.

When have I felt truly alive? How comfortable or uncomfortable am I when considering my own death?

Day 307

Standing in the Breach

Jesus' final and most important lesson from the cross was to teach humanity how to hold the middle and fill the tragic gaps of history by some cost to ourselves—instead of always asking others to pay the price. Consider the cross as a geometric symbol. Jesus hangs at the intersection of opposing forces and pays the price in his own body for their reconciliation (Ephesians 2:13–18).

Whenever you try to hold things together—to build a bridge or be a bridge—you will suffer. When you refuse to hide in either security camp—the ideologies of Left or Right, black or white, Christian or Jew, American or Arab, gay or straight—be prepared to "be hated by all" (Matthew 10:22) and, like Jesus, to have "nowhere to lay [your] head" (Luke 9:58). To live the mystery of the cross often means that you please no one, in hopes of healing everyone.

What costs have I suffered when trying to be a bridge?

Day 308

Building Bridges

Jesus probably never used the term *bridge builder*, but that's what he was with Jews and Samaritans, so-called healthy and so-called sinners, insiders and outsiders. We cannot build a bridge from the middle; we have to start on one side or the other. Jesus illustrates that we must build a bridge from the side of the disempowered ones. There we must first find our solidarity, and that is why he always went to the edges of his own religion and society. This comes to us as a true divine revelation because culture would never have led us to this conclusion. In fact, every culture I know of disagrees with this in practice.

Jesus always stands on the side of the outsider. He starts on the side of the losers, the victims, and the powerless; on the side of women who have been abused and oppressed by their patriarchal culture; on the side of gentiles in his Jewish culture or sinners in the Pharisaic culture.

If I am ready to build bridges, on which side am I standing right now?

Day 309

Facing Our Death

It is important to overcome our resistance to death—ahead of time—or we'll never take seriously this one limited life. This may explain why Jesus sought out and submitted to John the Baptist's offbeat death and transformation ritual at the Jordan River. It also explains why Paul still understood baptism as being buried with Jesus "into death" (Romans 6:4). It was only later that we watered it down into a pretty christening ceremony for children.

Three times in the Gospel of Mark, Jesus talked to the disciples about the necessity of facing death (8:31—10:45). And three times they changed the subject, missed the point, or actively opposed him. And these were the twelve apostles! This is probably why he finally stopped talking about it and just did it; not ritually but really. This is surely why death and resurrection, what Christians call the "paschal mystery," lie at the heart of every Eucharist, regardless of the feast or season. It takes many years and many seasons to overcome our resistance to, and our denial of, certain death.

How do I resist talking about death or even thinking about it?

Day 310

What It Takes to Be Saved

Even though we come up with multiple ways to deny it, the transformation of every death into some kind of resurrection is the core lesson of a man's spiritual journey. Rebirth is the only way we are "saved," to use a term that sometimes embarrasses us. For some reason, we have become content with our unhappiness, cynicism, fear, and alienation. But *salvation is always sickness turned around and upside down*. It is not just sickness and sin perfectly and forever avoided.

Jesus never once asked us to worship him; he asked us only to follow him in this constant transformation of death into newer and ever deeper forms of life. Far too often, our repetitive worship has become a clever avoidance of our following Jesus' path. He says as much to James and John when they try to secure for themselves thrones rather than drink "the cup that I drink" (Mark 10:35–40).

Do I have any sense that I need to be saved, and if so, from what? Have I settled for a lesser life that requires no transformation, or am I willing to die and live again?

DAY 311
NO SHAME

When we embrace our inner poverty of spirit, as Jesus recommended in Matthew 5:3, we embrace the limited, shadowy, and shamed parts of our selves. Until we can embrace that which we fear the most, we will live at some level of dissatisfaction and forever feel that we are not quite good enough. Or we will "split" and try to pretend it is not true, seeking out all kinds of diversionary tactics so we will not see that which is unacceptable to us or to others.

Some people tend to follow the path of self-doubt, while others follow the path of denial and diversion. Both groups lose, and the only way out for either of us is to follow Jesus' advice that he began with: "How happy are the poor in spirit!" These alone have nothing to prove and nothing to protect. These alone enjoy "the freedom of the glory of the children of God" (Romans 8:21). What else would inner freedom mean?

Where is poverty most apparent in my life?

DAY 312

WE TWO BEING ONE ARE WHOLE

Because so much of the world's population is rightly angry at patriarchy, many people are not free to recognize the good power of masculinity. Masculinity is not the same as patriarchy. Maleness, we must remember, is half of the mystery of God (Genesis 1:27). But what exactly does good maleness look like?

My personal opinion is this: the male principle (which is found in men and women) is that part of you that protects separateness, autonomy, and the whole. The male principle is the guardian of dignity, integrity, and solitude. Without it, we have only enmeshment and messiness in thought, word, and action.

But these qualities make sense only when joined with the female principle, which is the part of human personality that protects relationship, connection, and the parts themselves. The female principle is the guardian of intimacy, goodness, and beauty. Without it, we have only coldness, analysis, and theories about everything.

Only when the masculine and feminine defer to each other and love each other, do we have people—or cultures—that are healthy and happy.

How have I integrated the feminine qualities
of being human?

Day 313

Jesus as Nonviolent Warrior

Jesus was not a soft, spineless man, though he's often portrayed that way. It would be hard for men to warm up to such a man, let alone choose to follow him. But if you look beyond the pastel portraits to the real events of Jesus' life, you'll discover a man who took an unwavering stand against human suffering and engaged in a focused, unapologetic battle with evil, sickness, and oppression. The focus with which he responded to his call, the ability he possessed to toughen himself alone in the desert, and his identification with good power show Jesus to be a defined warrior.

When he says, "I have not come to bring peace, but a sword" (Matthew 10:34), he shows that he is not afraid of power, especially the more courageous power of nonviolence, which Martin Luther King, Jr. said is not for cowards. Jesus speaks of the sword, but then he utterly redefines it on his own terms, which is clear from the Sermon on the Mount and from his attitude before, during, and after his own murder.

Where is the positive warrior energy in my life?
When have I used that energy wrongly?

Day 314

The Way of the Warrior

J esus could refuse to answer phony or disingenuous questions. He bravely marched into the temple to demonstrate against religious practices gone awry. He didn't run from the agony he faced in the Garden of Gethsemane. He endured his night of torture and humiliation without losing heart or becoming violent in return. He remained faithful to love even through his execution.

Jesus turned nonviolent resistance into an art form, mainly by *ignoring* the Roman occupiers rather than engaging them directly. When you fight anything directly, especially for too long, you become a mirror image of it. Jesus confronted the necessary controversies wisely and calmly when he needed to. He could also be silent, leave the room, or change the question when he saw that confrontation was useless. His ability to endure his death with dignity and freedom reveals a warrior of the first magnitude. And of course, the long-lasting result was that he won! In fact, we Christians call it "the salvation of the world." Yet few Christians have imitated his tactic, his style, and his clear agenda for winning.

What aspect of Jesus' warrior quality do I most need to develop right now?

Day 315

Jesus as Wise Man

The archetypal wise man is not the quick-answer man but the one who leads others toward depth and wisdom. The wise man—sometimes known as the magician or the trickster—serves as the agent of transformation, but in roundabout ways! In the accounts of his life, Jesus certainly exemplifies this kind of wise man. His teaching is much more alternative than conventional wisdom. He uses riddles, parables, and not-so-clear aphorisms to open up our quality of seeing and hearing.

Yet in his lifetime, Jesus' teaching held enough compelling authority to move people to leave everything and follow him. Unfortunately, we have a tendency to look to Jesus for quick and final answers to everything rather than demonstrations of process and journey. We have demanded an easy "what" from Jesus, when, like all wise men, he is teaching us primarily "how." Did you know that according to several scholars, Jesus *directly* answers only three of the 183 questions asked of him in the four Gospel accounts? In fact, usually he created dilemmas for us that required wisdom and transformation.

What questions do I keep asking Jesus, hoping for quick and final answers?

Day 316

OUR PREFERENCE FOR KINGS

The human ego feels more comfortable with kings than with wise men. It prefers answer givers over spiritual guides. Kings give rulings that must bring clarity and order; spiritual guides invite us into the messiness of our interior lives and most social issues. Wise men must reveal the shadow sides of their kingdoms, which CEOs, heads of state, and bishops usually cannot or will not do.

Isn't it interesting that, in the retelling of the story of Jesus' birth, we turned the magi/astrologers into "three kings" even though there is no evidence in the text to justify that switch? That's a clear indication of just how much we fear wise men and prefer kings. The best way to keep a whistle-blower from blowing his whistle is to promote him or give him a big title or a raise in pay. Company men cannot speak against the company. Wise men are never mere company men.

How can I tell when I am avoiding wisdom by going to authority?

Day 317

Prophets Are without Honor

We also prefer kings to prophets. Prophets speak the truth, and hardly anyone is comfortable with that.

The prophet is the highest form of the magician or wise man archetype, who tells the truth no matter what the cost. Although thousands of churches are named "Christ the King," you'd be hard put to find one named "Christ the Prophet" anywhere in the world. At least I never have. That's how much we fear prophets, but *prophet* is a title that Jesus never rejected or denied, and even claimed as his dishonored position (Mark 6:4).

The New Testament Scriptures twice list prophet as the second most important role for building up the church (Ephesians 4:11; 1 Corinthians 12:28), yet there has never been a place for such a role in organized Christianity since we became the established religion of the Roman Empire in 313. Strange, and yet not so strange at all.

Who are the prophets in my life? Who are the wise men?

Day 318

Jesus as Archetypal Lover

The foundational meaning of Jesus' healing ministry is that he—and by implication, God—does not like human suffering and is willing to enter into it and alleviate it. Jesus' surrender and forgiveness on the cross provide the Western psyche powerful symbols of sacrificial love. Why, then, have we preferred to depict him in art as a stately king on his throne, a lawgiver with his book, or the warrior judging nations with sword in hand? Only in recent times did we dare present him as "the sacred heart" or "the divine mercy" or the gentle Jesus knocking at the soul's door.

Jesus' capacity for loving compassion is what we enjoy and most need from him—because it's what we most desire and need from God. Judgments, laws, and threats do not heal the human heart, nor do they begin to reveal the depths of God's saving desire and intention (See Romans 11:33–36 or Colossians 2:2–3).

When have I witnessed true compassion and acceptance in another man?

Day 319

Everything Belongs

Jesus' central theme is the "kingdom of God." "King" is simply another name for father or grandfather energy, the strong and stable male that can hold together chaos, fear, and doubt inside a larger goodness and greatness. When a good dad is home, the house is safe and secure, psychologically and physically. When Jesus merely enters the house, people are healed and their demons flee. This is the inherent power of the good father and the good king. Jesus, the ultimate "king of kings," can bring together all the seeming opposites, overcome the contradictions, and therefore forgive everything. The king is that part of you who can do the same with all the disparate parts of your own soul, both your good and your bad—along with the good and bad of others.

Jesus invites everyone to his banquet feast, "both good and bad" (Matthew 22:10). Your inner king is that part of you that doesn't need to exclude anyone or anything. The king is strong enough, big enough, and spacious enough to allow everything to "belong."

Who, if anyone, has served in my life as father-king? What have I learned about how to be an inner king, one who makes life stable for others?

DAY 320

TO PARTICIPATE IN GOD'S LIFE

The core, authentic goal of Christianity is to lead people to "become participants of the divine nature" (2 Peter 1:4). Only the Eastern Church had the courage to speak without apology of the goal as "divinization," what they called *theosis*. The Western Church—Catholic and Protestant—made Christian life into a laborious process of private morality in which very few could succeed. This reflected our more rational and mechanic approach to religion.

Once you realize that participating in God's nature is the whole point, you will see it described in a thousand ways in John's Gospel and most of the letters of the New Testament, which often reflect that more mystical level of Jesus' teaching. Remember, we are not talking about moral perfection, emotional maturity, or even psychological wholeness. The divinization process is participation with the very life of God. The way the Bible usually stated it was just that we are "sons of God," even "beloved sons"! Our DNA is objectively divine, even though we remain quite human. Please trust me on this one—it's the biggie!

What do I really believe about sharing in the divine nature?

Day 321

Grand Theater

What if the way to transmute the pain of life is to reveal the wounded side of all things, *and yet place such wounds inside a larger sacred and healing space?* Stories of wars, massacres, adulteries, betrayals, rapes, deceit, injustice, and greed, ending with the bloody crucifixion, fill the Bible. But let's consider that these stories are designed precisely to help us name, face, integrate, and forgive the wounds and sins of history. Somehow God is involved even in the mud and mess of it all. This strategy for dealing with darkness is quite different from that of excluding problems or denying difficulties or separating from sinners. It *includes* them instead, and says that God is still here! God's agenda is never elimination but transformation.

Soon the Bible becomes utterly honest and healing theater. It leaves the whole drama on the stage to reveal life as it is—to be observed, recognized, critiqued, loved, healed, and forgiven—all inside of the Unified Field that we call "God."

What wound do I urgently need to place
in sacred space?

Day 322

The Perfect Is the Enemy of the Good

For humans, true and full goodness is a mistake transformed rather than a mistake always avoided. Goodness is often and usually "the art of the possible" given this unique situation. Goodness is not pushing the heroic limits nearly as much as gracefully living inside the limits.

Religious people have a habit of confusing the perfect with the good, and often end up achieving neither. Because they cannot do the perfect thing they do nothing, or they criticize others who are not perfect. In both cases, they miss out on simple and always-possible human goodness.

Perfection is not available to us. God alone is perfect, and yet Jesus left perfection to share in our human imperfection. He needed to show us that the human situation is not all bad and actually an arena for the good! Too often our egoistic and heroic desire for the perfect becomes the major enemy of the good—what we could do right now, right here, and in this always imperfect situation.

How has perfectionism—mine or someone else's—
affected my life so far?

DAY 323

CAN GOD SUFFER?

We look for something certain, strong, undying, and infinite. Religion tells us that this something is what we mean by God. Then Jesus comes along and says, in effect, *But I suffer. I participate fully in the poverty and powerlessness of this world* (Philippians 2:6–8). So who is God? How do we put these contradictory and exclusive images of God together? Jesus is offered as the living paradox in which all the oppositions of the mind collide, and he holds all the contradictions together within himself (Colossians 1:20). He is the bush that burns yet is not consumed, the lamb slain yet victorious, a powerless Power, an Omnipotence that still "suffers," Eternal Divine Spirit that has become physical, concrete, and so ordinary.

The best invitation into this eternally suffering God is to suffer too and hold our own paradoxes and contradictions gracefully. Thereafter, God will not be an abstract philosophical idea, but *like will know like*, and God's heart will find a place inside ours.

**What can I learn from Jesus about
the finiteness of life?**

Day 324

Domination Just Delays the Problem

Denying, hating, or trying to separate from the negative never makes the negative go away; it merely postpones or displaces it temporarily. We can't "solve" evil by condemning it and then legislating against it. In Romans and Galatians, Paul unpacks this dilemma, saying that the law is merely "our disciplinarian" to get us started on the path (Galatians 3:24). Law can give us information and social order, but not what God is holding out for—*the actual transformation of free persons into divine love.*

Domination *over* things is quite different from transformation *of* things, and in the midst of their good intentions, people often confuse the two. Grace and love can happen only in realms of freedom. This is God's agenda. It's an immense risk on God's part, seems not to be working most of the time, and yet it is clear that God continues to take that risk. God's great plan must indeed be the actual transformation of persons into free and loving partners of the Godhead.

When have I tried to dominate my way to a better situation? What happened?

Day 325

The Two Great Commandments

When we idealize anything, we end up idol-izing it. We infatuate, which means a "false fire," and eventually burn out. We attach to our idol unreal expectations and become disappointed, feeling betrayed.

Likewise, when we see anything as totally bad, we allow it to have far too much power over us. So we try to fight it directly, which eventually leads to our taking on its dark power and becoming its mirror image. We don't see this and thus become hypocrites, fanatics, and insufferable religious types (Matthew 7:4–5).

The two great commandments provide a way through both these illusions. If we worship God alone, then we allow nothing else to infatuate us for long. If we love others as we love ourselves, and even extend that to the enemy, then there is no room for moral crusades against evil "out there." It takes all our moral energy, and then some, to deal with all the obstacles to love "in here."

What have I idolized? What expectations are pushing me toward disappointment?

Day 326

Healthy Warrior Energy

We cannot take the testosterone out of men—nor should we want to. Instead, we must claim that energy for larger purposes than tribal games and group security needs. Martin of Tours, Francis of Assisi, Ignatius of Loyola, and Charles de Foucauld never stopped being knights and soldiers. They discovered the true meanings of the warrior. They discovered the dark side of their warrior and learned from it. We must name and rightly initiate the warrior archetype or else he remains petty, violent, and unaccountable to self or society. If we don't work with these primal energies within men, they will work against us.

Strangely enough, many young men take pride in being taught discipline, focus, respect, boundaries, and self-denial. They run to coaches, bosses, and drill sergeants as if to beloved father figures. The young man knows he needs discipline yet knows it has to be forced on him because he cannot do it for himself. His unconscious and the Holy Spirit must be guiding him toward what he needs.

Where do I turn for training to be a good warrior?

Day 327

Loose Cannons

The man has to embody his aggressiveness and recognize how far it can lead him—and where it will fail him. He has to experience in his body the difference between good anger, narcissistic reaction, and egocentric rage.

Nonviolence does not come easily or naturally. Even peace work can be a cover for the dark warrior, and I have met "peace and justice people" who've never faced their needs for power and control. I've known military men more in charge of their aggressiveness than are many church folks and peaceniks. This is why we all need to do our spiritual work, and why spirituality is much more demanding than merely adopting a positive image, title, or job description, such as peace worker or soldier.

If we don't initiate the positive warrior in a man, the dark warrior in some form will take over. And aggressiveness in most men will not just go away. We either educate warrior energy or we'll have loose cannons firing aimlessly in all directions.

How can I tell the difference, from my personal experience, between good anger and egocentric rage?

Day 328

Wise Guys

All higher forms of prayer are designed to help us go beyond the limited rational mind which cannot process things like spirituality or suffering, mystery or God. *Faith and prayer are not so much for the overcoming of obstacles as they are for the experiencing of them.* Then they teach us whatever they have to teach us.

The mind is often a wonderful doorway into experience, but it can also be a primary barrier to it. If we do not both validate and then challenge the skills of the mind, we will never go beyond knowledge of facts and data to the wide eyes of wisdom. This process of prayer beyond the mind is called contemplation or meditation. Contemplation greases our wheels in the wild rides through suffering and absurdity. It is the necessary ground of any spirituality worthy of the name, and it is the fully open horizon that allows us to love and trust mystery. Thus a wise man never stops growing and never ceases to enjoy life.

Where do I see my mind helping me on the spiritual journey? Where do I see it getting in the way of wisdom?

Day 329

Holy Bewilderment

A true wise man has the willingness—and the ability—to stand comfortably between knowing and not knowing, between so-called darkness and what seems like light. That is what makes him wise instead of merely intelligent. Did you ever notice that Paul lists preaching with wisdom and preaching instruction as two distinct and different gifts of the Spirit (1 Corinthians 12:8). In other words, a wise man is not just an intelligent man; wisdom is actually a different way of accessing your information. I like to call it "non-dualistic" knowing, which always leaves room for a third or fourth alternative and possibility.

Victor Frankl, the brilliant Jewish psychologist and Holocaust survivor, wrote, "Sell your cleverness and purchase bewilderment instead!" It is our willingness and freedom to live with a certain kind of bewilderment that characterizes the true wise man. He forever has a "beginner's mind" that keeps him humble, human, and honest.

When am I best able to know that I don't know?

Day 330

You Don't Say!

One trait that usually characterizes wise men is the tendency to be quiet. They wait and listen. They speak only when they have something to say. As we grow older, we should aspire to that kind of calm and natural discernment—not to squelch our expression but to refine it so that when we speak, it is the best we have to offer. People know the difference when we are just thinking out loud, and when we actually have something to say.

There are three gates through which a wise man's words must pass:

+ The first gate: Is what I'm saying really true? If it's not true, then, of course, don't bother.
+ The second gate: Is it loving? Am I about to say something that will build up life and trust, or will it tear them down?
+ The third gate (and probably the most difficult): Is what I am about to say really that necessary? If it's not, why clutter up the moment with more words and noise competing for space and attention?

As I look back on what I've said today, how would my speech pass through these three gates?

Day 331

Blessed Joy, Blessed Pleasure

The lover archetype is that part of a man that enjoys the simple pleasures of life—the healthy enjoyments of relationship, work, home, nature, and daily things. We are not comfortable with real lover energy, although we think we are. Unless it is a spectacle and spectacular, we don't access our love energy. The true lover will allow a leaf or a smile to give him joy.

We create empty substitutes for these daily pleasures. But if *you do not truly enjoy little things, you will barely enjoy the big things*. Enjoyment is a skill we practice every moment until it becomes a way of life.

Isn't it strange that Western culture breeds conspicuous consumerism while taking Jesus, a poor and simple man, as its primary hero and God figure? It would make more sense, according to our actual value system, if our God figure were Dionysus or Pan. It seems to take higher and higher levels of stimulation and entertainment to make us feel alive. This means that the lover archetype is dying within us.

*How can I receive this life and enjoy
its true pleasures?*

Day 332

Recreation Is to Re-Create Us

When it comes to the lover archetype, most of us are out of balance. We feel guilty about delight and pleasure, even though Jesus never indicated that they were evil. At the same time, we turn to the physical world for our daily pleasures but seldom allow them to bring us closer to God, to ourselves, or to one another. Sensual experiences have become mere diversions and distractions instead of deep moments of connection and communion.

When body and spirit are operating as one, a true sexual encounter, a loving meal, or a slow walk in the garden is much more Godly than a perfectly orthodox religious ceremony that is done with a cold, impersonal, or disconnected heart. You'd think that Christianity would prefer the lover archetype over the warrior, sage, or king, but for some reason we have mistrusted it and remained split from it, while still daring to enjoy it. The contemplative is the highest level of the lover; he is able to find joy and love everywhere he turns.

How do I imagine God seeing my sexuality?

Day 333

Make Room for Eros

If religion does not integrate and validate the sensual, pleasure-loving, erotic aspect of the personality, it will go in devious and destructive directions. If we do not bless and respect our sexuality, it will turn on and control us. Dom Bede Griffiths said, "Sex is far too important to eliminate entirely, and it is far too important to do lightly. The only alternative is to somehow consecrate it."

The most loving men in life, and the most generous to society, usually possess a lusty sense of beauty, pleasure, and sex—but they have realistic and healthy expectations. They know that smaller pleasures offer a taste that creates hunger for something more and eternal. This is the necessary training of the lover archetype in all of us. Quite simply, if you know how to love others, you will also know how to love God, and how to let God love you. *How you do sex is a good indicator of how you do relationship in general*, and how you do relationship is how you will connect—or not connect—with God and everything else.

In what ways do I appreciate and integrate the sensual and erotic? What expectations do I have of the erotic?

Day 334

Bringing It All Together

The king archetype or energy holds together the warrior, the wise man, and the lover in a grand display of balance and wholeness. The healthy king also comprehends his own limits, and he can even risk looking powerless. True kings do not have to walk around wearing uniforms, badges, and special hats to convince others of who they are. Their authority comes from within and from their proven record of accomplishments.

Such kingship is rare, which is why we must name it and present it as the ultimate male goal. The king is not just a good leader or a benevolent father. Simply by walking around, such a man is our contact with the holy and universal. He tells us that wholeness and holiness are possible, just as Nelson Mandela and Desmond Tutu still do for South Africa. Recently I returned from a preaching tour in Capetown, and their continued influence is everywhere, even though they are old retired men. Their energy is not retired at all!

*How far have I journeyed in becoming
a true king?*

Day 335

The King and His Kingdom

Saul, Herod, Pilate, Stalin, and Hitler are examples of the dark king. There seems to be no end to them in history. These men hold no vision of the whole, no great realm to hold together. Yet they often appeal to people at their level of moral development. Their only realm is their own small kingdom and their personal self-interest. In democratic countries, we often see politicians who seem to have no other concern than getting reelected. And yet people whose kingdoms are also small will keep reelecting them! Almost as if we cannot imagine a bigger picture ourselves.

The dark king excludes and eliminates his enemies. The true king, like Nelson Mandela, invites his jailers to his inauguration or, like Abraham Lincoln, who in attempting to heal the nation after the American Civil War, calls the people to show "malice toward none and charity toward all." Jesus says from the cross, "Father, forgive them; for they do not know what they are doing" (Luke 23:34).

In my own life, who has served as dark king,
and who as the good king?

Day 336

A King and a Cobbler

A young prince needs healthy models and mentors along the way if he is to become a good king. He needs to meet passionate lovers, truly wise men, and warriors who've fought both their inner and outer demons. If he learns from them, he will be prepared to hold together his own realm in time. He will be a king, even if only in his chosen area of competence.

You can be the king of the cobbler shop, and people will come from miles around to your cobbler court simply to be seen and blessed. You will not only repair their shoes but also mend their souls—and they may not even know that's why they came. I hope you all have met such a man. They are hidden away everywhere with usually no need to be seen or to become famous. They reign by being.

What is my personal court like where people come to me, where I have the potential to be a true king?

Day 337

Survival Dance to Sacred Dance

Nothing fresh or creative is likely to happen when life is going smoothly. Nothing original or creative emerges from the status quo or business as usual. The structure we create in the first half of life can become a prison in the second half of life, if we do not move beyond it. The initial building of our "house" is what Bill Plotkin calls our "survival dance."

In the second half of life, we have a different spiritual agenda. Rather than building up and acquiring, we need to learn to let go. Often it takes a crisis of some magnitude before we are willing to do this. Thus our sacred dance begins when we allow our newly discovered soul to draw us forward. The first house has been the platform and foundation—on which we can finally and fully do the dance for which we were really created.

Have I begun to let go? If so, what has happened to bring about this willingness?

DAY 338

WHERE'S THE JOY?

M en often report that they find it hard to hear God. But truthfully, it is harder *not* to hear God. The pain of living unaware of God's presence is greater and more pervasive than the fleeting discipline of opening mind, heart, and soul to Mystery. Those who have had an immediate experience of God have tasted peace, delight, even ecstasy. Why? Because that is what we were made for! One must work pretty hard—against negativity and inner resistance— to block out God's obvious presence in all things.

If your life has no deep joy, inherent contentment, or warm devotion, then it's not authentic experience of soul or of the divine. If the primary flavor of your religion is fear, or if it is mainly a series of religious duties and obligations, then it's hardly worth your while—and may be part of the problem. Helen Keller, the blind and deaf woman who achieved such a high level of love and consciousness, said, "It has crossed my mind that much religion may perhaps be man's despair at *not* finding God!"

Where is the joy in my life?

DAY 339

YOU ALREADY ARE SOMEBODY

The commonly held myth of the self-made man is a trap. The idea that we can manufacture our own identity or worthiness is a project sure to fail. Thinking that we can and must create our own significance turns every other man into a rival and leaves us fighting over the scraps.

The soul lives on meaning the way the body lives on food. Without a larger meaning, our lives are "disasters," which literally means "disconnected from the stars"! It is absolutely essential that we find this larger meaning. Jesus has already declared you inherently important: "Rejoice that your names are written in heaven," he says (Luke 10:20). You cannot declare yourself important; any attempt to do so is delusional, even though many try. The problem we try so hard to solve is already completely solved, and most of us don't even know it. We are searching for what we already have.

In what ways do I still strive to be a self-made and worthy man?

Day 340

Redemptive Suffering

The suffering of Jesus shows us that God is not distanced from humanity's trials. Our Creator does not heal our suffering from afar but participates with us in it. In fact, the great revelation signified in Jesus is not only that God participates in our suffering, but also that our suffering has life-giving elements for the evolution of humanity, or what I call "Christ consciousness" (Ephesians 4:23–24).

The primary story line of history has been one of "redemptive violence"; the killing of others would supposedly save and protect us. Jesus introduced and lived a new story line of "redemptive suffering"; our suffering for others and for the world makes a difference in the greater scheme. No love is lost in the universe, but it is building up and helping to create the eternal Christ consciousness. As Paul so courageously and trustfully puts it, "I am now rejoicing in my sufferings for your sake, and in my flesh I am completing what is lacking in Christ's afflictions for the sake of his body, that is, the church" (Colossians 1:24).

What do I suffer today? Where might God be in that suffering?

Day 341

Mr. Lightbulb

Great people are usually humble. They understand and accept that they draw from another Source; they are satisfied to be an instrument. Their genius is not of their own making but a gift. They do great things precisely because they do not take first or final responsibility for their gift, and they don't worry much about their failures. They understand that their life is not their own but has been entrusted to them. Someone Else has taken them seriously, and they feel profoundly respected, which is what men ultimately want and need.

A few weeks ago I was invited to meet with Archbishop Desmond Tutu in Capetown, South Africa. He told me that he—and I—were mere lightbulbs. We get all the credit and seem to be shining brightly for all to see, but we both know that if this lightbulb was unscrewed from its source for even a moment, the brightness would immediately stop. He laughed hilariously afterwards, and gave me a wink of understanding!

Where is the abundance in my life? And how do
I pass it along to others?

Day 342

It's Enough to Be You

Shortly before dying, St. Francis told his band of broth-ers, "I have done what is mine to do. Now you must do what is yours to do." Great people do not need to concoct an identity or a brand for themselves.

"The work" is merely to discover and enjoy the identity you already have. And yet many of us find it hard simply to be who we are; it feels too little, too ordinary. But God only expects you to be who you really are. That's why the most courageous thing you might ever do is to accept yourself and be that man, and no other. I tried for years to be St. Francis until I realized that this is what he encouraged me *not* to be! I am not to be St. Francis or Mother Teresa or any other idealized hero. My job is simply to be Richard, warts and all. This is so much harder, and takes so much more trust and surrender. But it's the giving of the whole self that matters, not the perfection of it.

What is mine to do in this life?

Day 343

At One End of Jacob's Ladder

In the spiritual life, what we think we are doing is actually being done to us; all we can do is say yes to it. You will one day find yourself inside the Other and held by the Other, your own glory intact and protected. Your true self will be revealed to you, and you will happily discover that it is much more glorious, grounded, original, and free than any identity you could devise for yourself. *More than finding it, you sort of find yourself falling into it, like falling in love.*

We are participating in the very life of God while living out one little part of that life in our own exquisite form. When the eureka moment ("I have found it") happens, you will be like Jacob awakening at the foot of the ladder to heaven, and you will join him in saying "You were here all the time, and I never knew it!"

What does it feel like to be found by God?
Can I recall a specific time when I was
acutely aware of that?

Day 344

Burned by God

After an authentic God experience, our lives are tinged with perpetual dissatisfaction. Nothing can totally satisfy us—not the church, our relationships, our country, our job, or ourselves. No matter who is president, popular, or pope, we'll be unhappy. This is radical, aching dissatisfaction. *Ordinary life will never again be good enough, and yet strangely it is more than enough.* The briefest, slightest encounter with God burns us, in a way. It introduces us to a strange kind of loneliness, because we've been touched by something we could never be ready for, something we cannot endure yet—still, we want more!

God is henceforth both perfectly hidden and perfectly revealed in everything. But much of the time, the divinity feels more hidden than revealed. It is a slow burn. This longing is holy and draws us inexorably toward the One whose touch first awakened us.

When have I experienced God in such a way that everything changed?

Day 345

The Burning Continues

A peak spiritual experience can be disconcerting. After the experience, you no longer fit in. You live the rest of your life out of step with the world, slightly off-center. What everyone else is getting excited about leaves you unfazed. You see the latest gadgets, events, elections, and sensational news items for what they are, mostly shadow and disguise. Why is everybody else so preoccupied with mere passing dramas? Don't they see? Don't they know? Am I crazy? Or are they crazy? Are we perhaps just crazy in different ways?

You can try to escape what you've come to know, but the ambush is set. The "Hound of Heaven" is after you and ever on your trail. You run away, deny, ignore, reject, and avoid too many times to count, but you know you will always come back. No other lover loves half as well.

Now that I understand life as more than honor,
power, or possessions, what is my story line,
the thing I seek?

Day 346

The Homing Device

It is God within you who loves God. By ourselves, we do not know how or where to look for God. We don't even know what God looks like. We don't know what to think—or if we should try to think at all.

God planted a little bit of God inside you—we call it the indwelling Holy Spirit (John 14:16–17)—and from that place within you, like a homing device, God seeks and loves God. It is happening to you, through you, toward you, within you, and from you. All you can do is allow the spring inside you to well up (John 4:14) and flow through you.

Go to this holy place within you, which is the only place big enough to allow you to encounter, hold, and bear the darkness.

When have I sensed God within me seeking God?

Day 347

Practical Next Steps

There are practical aspects and strategies for staying on the path of transformation:

+ Read good books, especially biographies of people you admire.
+ Watch movies, gaze at art, listen to music.
+ Pay attention to your dreams, where your archetypes reveal themselves.
+ Pray and meditate regularly, to clean the lens so the images of soul can appear.
+ Learn from the negative archetypes as well as the positive.
+ Make use of practices that move you to the right brain, where your soul can speak to you more spontaneously.
+ Spend a lot of time in nature.
+ Keep a journal. But write in an uncensored way, not for anyone else to read.

How do I go to the place where the soul can speak?

Day 348

Wrestling with the Angel

The point of the journey is to enter a wrestling match with the same angel that wrestled with Jacob (Genesis 32:23). We will become wounded as Jacob did, or discover the wound that was always there; but now we know that the wound was given by God. We will spend the rest of our lives limping, yet the limp will not hamper us, but in fact will be the blessing.

Wounded men like Jacob, who have let their wounds become blessings, learn to speak the paradoxical language of the soul. Once we touch upon the blessing of this encounter, we will start using words in different ways. Fundamentalist literalism will feel like a major regression and a limitation. *Once deep wounds have become greatest blessings, all language is inadequate to describe your new world of paradox and mystery.* Once our wounds become sacred wounds, it will be like learning a new language.

What is this spiritual journey for me right now?

Day 349

Any Saint Jesus?

Stories of men with tragic flaws, backtracking, blind spots, denials, and betrayals fill the Scriptures; in fact, they are the norm. Think of Adam, Jacob and Esau, Moses, David, Solomon, Peter and Paul. Yet they were used by God, each in his own way part of the divine plan. I can't think of a single biblical male who would make it through Rome's canonization process today. Even Jesus never would have become "Saint Jesus" because of his theological confusions and loophole-filled moral principles.

Furthermore, none of us lives half the truth we do know. Still, we know it's the truth, and it keeps edging us forward with holy discomfort. As Jeremiah says, "There is something like a burning fire shut up in my bones, and the effort to restrain it wearies me" (Jeremiah 20:9). We are trapped and enclosed within a bigger truth that we cannot endure or live up to. Yet it keeps inviting us through the unbelievably patient voice of God. *You do not need to get to the North Star to be totally guided by it.*

What truth do I know, and how am I trying to live up to it?

Day 350

The Face of the Other

In the book of Job, God makes no attempt to respond to Job's concerns, point by point, because such answers will never satisfy him anyway. Only "the voice from the whirlwind," the encounter itself will change him. In the Gospels, Jesus usually remains silent before his antagonists or simply refuses to entertain their hostile questions. He often tries to reframe or redirect the question, to force them toward the big questions—for which Presence is the only satisfying response. "Let your face shine upon us and we will be satisfied" (Psalm 80:9).

We could look at the central theme of the Bible as calling people to constant encounters with the face of otherness: the sinner, the stranger, the alien, the Samaritan, the Gentile, the poor, the handicapped, even our own hidden and denied faces. These become practice encounters that prepare us for a major Encounter. If we don't let other people change us here, if we are not vulnerable before the needs of others, why would we change when we meet God?

How can I practice openness to others and to a world outside my own?

Day 351

Evil Is Neither First nor Last

Evil and sin are real and painful, but they are not decisive. They are neither the foundational nor the final truth. This is actually Christianity's major message! Genesis began by saying that all creation "was good" from the very beginning (1:10+), and then the resurrection of the crucified Jesus was God's promise to humanity that the final chapter of all human crucifixions will also be resurrection! Even on the unconscious level, the worldview in which you live is "saving" you and taking away your anxiety, self-doubt, and the sense of not belonging to something more. Sometimes I think that most "salvation" is happening most effectively on the unconscious level.

God's grace and mercy will have the last, final, and definitive word. We are not more powerful than God. "He will wipe away all tears from our eyes. There will be no more death, and no more mourning or sadness. The world of the past will be gone" says the final pages of the Bible (Revelation 21:4).

What is the most astounding grace I have experienced this week?

Day 352

What Hospice and Bereavement Teach Us

In the second half of life, suffering becomes an increasingly constant companion by reason of deaths, greater awareness of others' pain, losses, and our aging body. All of this lets us know that suffering is never just about us. It's our opportunity to hand on life and strength to our children, friends, and all those around us. In fact, in most of history *aging and death were a central spiritual event that educated the whole family, since the extended family lived together. Now aging, suffering, and death have become largely medical events,* and often separate and sanitized events in institutions. People die filled with tubes and pills, so they themselves are not conscious, nor can they pass on the wisdom that often only comes at the end. My mother was clearly looking at my "guardian angel" to the left of me three days before she died, and she was no pious Catholic who tended to see such things. She said it so matter-of-factly and clearly that I knew she was already passing through the veil.

What has suffering taught me this year?

Day 353

Knowledge without Faith

The saints and the Scriptures tell us there is no true wisdom without faith. Consider this:

1. We start with information, a combination of facts and data.
2. We place the data in larger frames, making more connections, and it becomes "knowledge."
3. We analyze it, and it becomes "intelligence."
4. We come to insight inside that intelligence, and we have "intuition," which is the source of most genius.
5. We connect our single field of discipline with other disciplines, and we have the beginnings of "understanding" the unified field.
6. We allow all of this "to rest in the largest conversation possible about things" and accept that *reality is both knowable and unknowable mystery*, while still honoring all the previous levels of knowledge. We can now see things nondualistically. "Transcend and Include" is now our style. Everything belongs. This is "wisdom"!

How do you move from one stage to the next? By letting go of total reliance upon the previous stage. To keep growing, you must endure darkness and self-doubt. The person who refuses to allow darkness and self-doubt will never move on.

When have I discovered, from hard experience,
that knowledge by itself is not enough?

Day 354

The Death Sentence

Allowing God to be God is not something a man does easily. It can take him a lifetime, and for this reason. Any movement toward divine union will always feel like a loss of self. And it is! But that is just because you are very attached to it—it is all you know at that point—and you are also habituated to it. We are victims of the familiar. It is your "false self" that you do not need anyway, but you don't know that yet.

Authentic conversion will always feel like dying, and if you are not trained in dying, it just will not happen—unless and until it's forced on you! You will remain your tiny "you" and God will remain "out there" and rather totally ineffective.

Unless this self dies, you cannot find yourself, and anyone who does lose this self will find himself, as Jesus tells us, several times, in different ways (e.g., Matthew 16:24). Jesus finally had to do it physically and personally, because there was so much resistance to the message.

As I move toward God, what am I afraid of losing?

Day 355

Let It Flow!

Men who actively draw upon the Divine Source know that they don't need to engineer their life or push their own agenda anymore. They may call it providence, destiny, or inner guidance, but they know that they are being led in a much better way than they could manage on their own. This is not provable to the logical mind, nor does it mean that we simply roll over and play dead. Receiving divine guidance is a very subtle and discreet art form that the Spirit teaches us by trial and error.

Surrendering to the divine flow is not about giving up, giving in, capitulating, becoming a puppet, being naive, being irresponsible, turning off your mind, or becoming someone you're not. Surrendering opens you up in a peaceful way that allows the conduit of "living water" to flow freely through you (John 7:38–39). Surrender is a willingness to trust that you are indeed a beloved son, which allows God to prove to you that he is indeed your loving Father.

When have I experienced true surrender? What keeps me from it now?

Day 356

Staring Down Death

In May of 1991 I was given a five-month life expectancy because of a skin cancer, malignant melanoma. I was not afraid of dying as much as desperately sad that this one great experiment and opportunity called my life was soon to be over. The love and prayers of many people must have healed me because I'm still here almost twenty years later. But afterward I was qualitatively different. Mostly, I knew I could and must speak my little bit of truth with whatever remaining days I had, and I knew that very few had been given the opportunities I had been given to do just that.

The big questions that emerge in the shadow of death are "Have I ever really loved?" and "Have I yet lived my real soul and destiny?" When we have loved honestly, we will have the courage to face death. And when we have faced death, we are free to live our deepest destiny, because ultimately that's all that we can offer back to life, to the universe, and to God.

*In what situation have I been closest to death,
and what did that do to me?*

Day 357

The Holy Fool

The experience of God is always an experience of totality. We feel a universal spaciousness. There is room for everything, and nothing needs to be excluded. Most of your judgments eventually seem so petty, unfounded, and self-referential. Your life is all unmerited grace, so why not everyone else's too? You stop weighing, counting, labeling, and measuring, because it makes no sense inside of universal and endless space.

This is why we often become holy fools in our later years. Like the trickster in many mythologies, we can stare down the dark side of things and not be threatened. This is hard to do when we're young men, in need of clear boundaries and definitions and unsure of what to do with our shadow. But as we get to be older men, and if we allow ourselves to grow wiser, we realize that anything can become a pathway to the Great Truth if it leads us to wonder. And the most urgent question of all—"Who am I?"—is, thank God, always answered, "God's beloved son."

Have I become a holy fool yet, or am I still clinging to boundaries and definitions?

Day 358

Forever

We carry within us a sense that we are meant for eternal life—an echo of something eternal; many call it the soul. Believers call it the indwelling presence of God. It is God in us who causes us to desire God. It is an eternal life already within us that sparks our awareness of such an impossible thing as eternal life. It is the Holy Spirit of God who allows us to seriously hope for what we only intuit.

We cannot imagine or hope for something if we haven't already touched on it in some small way. All spiritual cognition is actually recognition. So many would not seek and hope for eternal life if it were not a reality—it's not wishful thinking as much as secondary thinking. God thought of it first and planted the desire in our hearts. That's the pattern we discover in prayer: God makes us think it is our thought when it is really God's thought! *God comes to us—as us.* Like a good wife, God allows men to think it's their idea!

What do I imagine in my life of the spirit?
What do I hope for?

Day 359

Laying Down One's Life

When we live in the economy of grace, we stop weighing behavior in terms of good, better, and best; we simply allow life—and the failure that's part of life—to happen. When we follow love to its logical conclusion, we experience suffering because love gives itself away to those it loves—but with a price. Laying down one's life for another is the definition of mature love, as Jesus makes clear (John 15:13).

This love is not sacrifice in a morbid sense. Sacrifice comes from *sacrum facere*, "to make sacred or holy." We make something holy by reconnecting it to the whole—by giving ourselves away to the other in the same way that God has given Godself to us. In suffering we share God's passion. We agree to participate in what God is already doing for the sake of love and universal life. It's important that we discern the difference between this self-giving and the fantastic heroics we often call sacrifice. One is the virtue of the young man; the other is the virtue of a mature man.

How has suffering in my life been made sacred?

Day 360

Only a Suffering God Can Save

If we are suffering, God is suffering, and when we suffer trustfully and consciously we are in solidarity with God. All our saints discovered this, which is why some of them appear almost masochistic in their readiness to suffer. It was their way of connecting with everything.

In so many of the world's mythologies, the wounded one is invariably the gift giver. He is a blind seer, a crippled speaker of truth, or a beggar who offers wisdom. The one who has suffered is the one who has universal compassion, who carries all and understands all. The afflicted one becomes the bearer of hope. No surprise that Christianity worships as its central icon a severely wounded man. Any God outside of or disconnected from suffering cannot possibly "save" the world from its primary dilemma and downfall. It has to be an inside job, which is the only way that things are healed, from the inside out and from the bottom up.

What does the suffering God look like to me?

Day 361

Tend Your Spirit

"Deep calls to deep" (Psalm 42:7).

The Spirit within you is what keeps you open to that which is transcendent, other, and always larger—that which we call God. Like a homing pigeon, the Holy Spirit in you seeks the Holy Spirit in God. The indwelling presence of God is like a built-in compass, your magnetic center that keeps pulling you toward truth, love, and life. It's an inner mirroring that keeps prompting and programming you in your deepest and truest self. You really have to work hard to avoid or deny so much that is working totally in your favor.

"God's love has been poured into our hearts through the Holy Spirit that has been given to us" (Romans 5:5).

Do I honor the Spirit within me? Am I open to its promptings?

DAY 362

THE LOVE CLOCK

People in ancient times dreamed of eternal life, and they tried in ritualistic ways to prepare for it—it's our "immortality instinct." We often sense a connection to loved ones who have died. We sense that love is also somehow eternal, and therefore maybe life is, too.

If you have ever moved in the realms of love, you know that it feels somehow *limitless, undeserved, and totally illogical.* Love leads us to levels of self-abandonment, and hints of joy, that are literally unbelievable, and unattainable any other way. If love has an eternal quality to it, if God is love itself, and if we are able to participate in both God and love, then it does follow that we might just be eternal too.

Love knows and recognizes Love. Timelessness within us connects with the Eternal outside of us. People who have loved deeply, and been loved deeply, know they have touched on the timeless, and dare to easily and almost naturally believe in eternal life.

What does my intuitive love tell me
about life and death?

Day 363

So You Want to Start a Revolution?

There is a welcome revolution in spirituality today, a return to what Jesus actually taught! For instance, that we come to God through our imperfections and wounds, not by moral achievements. How have we missed such an obvious message? Is it just too good to be true? Do we prefer that the gospel be a win/lose scenario? Are we afraid of such a level playing field, knowing that all of us are saved by mercy?

At the heart of male spirituality is the knowledge that we are imperfect, that *we come to God not by doing it right, but ironically and wonderfully by doing it wrong!* In the end, God gets all the credit. If men have abandoned the churches of the world, it's because of a certain aversion to hypocrisy. They know they cannot be perfect, so they just opt out of the whole thing. More transformation is taking place in the Wednesday night church basements, with things like twelve-step meetings, than in Sunday morning sanctuaries where people are urged to compete in worthiness contests they cannot win.

Am I free to journey through my woundedness to God? What stands in the way?

Day 364

A Few Simple Things

In the end, a healthy man's life comes down to a few simple things.

+ If you want others to be more loving toward you, choose to love first.
+ If you want a peaceful outer world, reconcile your own inner world.
+ If you are tired of cynicism and negativity out there, cultivate hope in here.
+ If you wish to find stillness in the world, find the calm within yourself.

Gandhi, of course, put it best of all: "Be the change you want to see in the world."

Transformed people transform people, and usually only as far as they themselves have been transformed. So the best thing you can do for your family and the world is to keep growing up yourself.

What is my work today for love, peace, and stillness?

Day 365

If You Want

Here are two principles of the spiritual life: *what you see is what you get*, and *what you seek is what you get.* Both beauty and darkness really are—first—in the eye of the beholder!

If you find yourself resenting the faults of others, try not resenting the same faults in yourself. If you work for justice, treat yourself fairly too. If the world seems desperate, let go of your own despair.

What do I seek, and what must I do?

Day 366

A New Economy of Grace

"All belong to you, and you belong to Christ, and Christ belongs to God" (1 Corinthians 3:22–23).

All a man can pass on is what he has become; that is your blessing and gift for your children, your wife, your neighborhood, and the next generation, "grace upon grace" (John 1:16). Divine love bestowed is repaid by love alone.

Our lives seem small and insignificant, yet one life is a significant piece of the eternal and cosmic Christ, a short moment of Incarnation that is building up the Body of God.

You belong to God's universe because *everything belongs*. Every part of you belongs, and no part need be rejected or denied, but only educated, healed, forgiven, and set free in new form. In fact, if we are to believe the Gospel we must treat the lesser parts with the greater care (1 Corinthians 12:23).

Nothing is ever wasted in God's economy. All is transformed. Grace is everywhere.

Am I brave enough to find God within me and own that great gift?

To Learn More about Richard Rohr's Ministry and Men as Leaders and Elders (M.A.L.Es)

Richard Rohr, ORM, is author of more than 20 books and extensive audio recordings and is a sought-after speaker worldwide.

Visit www.cacradicalgrace.org to purchase books and audios, or to learn about upcoming speaking engagements or events featuring Richard Rohr.

 **Men as Leaders and Elders (M.A.L.Es)** offers Men's Rites of Passage along with resources on male spirituality and networking opportunities. To learn more about these programs or to find out what is going on in your region visit www.malespirituality.org.

 The Center for Action and Contemplation, founded by Richard Rohr in 1987, serves as agent and support for the ministry of Richard Rohr, and houses the Men as Leaders and Elders program. The Center, located in Albuquerque, New Mexico, is committed to providing experiential education that encourages the transformation of human consciousness through contemplation, equipping people to be instruments of peaceful change in the world. For more information about CAC or to participate in upcoming programs visit www.cacradicalgrace.org. or call (505) 242-9588.